What French Women Know

What French Women Know

ABOUT LOVE, SEX AND OTHER
MATTERS OF HEART AND MIND

DEBRA OLLIVIER

piatkus

PIATKUS

First published in the US in 2009 by G.P. Putnam's Sons, Penguin Group (USA) Inc.
First published in Great Britain in 2009 by Piatkus
This paperback edition published in 2010 by Piatkus
Reprinted 2010

A CIP catalogue record for this book
is available from the British Library.

ISBN 978-0-7499-5234-1

Text design by Nicole Laroche
Printed and bound in Great Britain by
Clays Ltd, St Ives plc

Papers used by Piatkus are natural, renewable and recyclable
products sourced from well-managed forests and certified
in accordance with the rules of the Forest Stewardship Council.

Mixed Sources
Product group from well-managed
forests and other controlled sources
www.fsc.org Cert no. SGS-COC-004081
© 1996 Forest Stewardship Council

Piatkus
An imprint of
Little, Brown Book Group
100 Victoria Embankment
London EC4Y 0DY

An Hachette UK Company
www.hachette.co.uk

www.piatkus.co.uk

It is good to know something of the customs of different people in order to judge more soundly of our own, and so that we might not think that all that which is contrary to our own ways be ridiculous and contrary to reason, as those who have seen nothing have the habit of doing.

—DESCARTES

Contents

Preface to the UK Edition

A word for my English and Commonwealth readers. Throughout this book, I've used the term "Anglo-Saxon" or "Anglo" as a multipurpose generic for American and British-flavored cultures—and for those individuals raised on such soil. I've done so well aware that the Normans conquered the Anglo-Saxons centuries ago, and that nobody speaks like Beowulf anymore. To linguistic purists bothered by this liberty, mea culpa.

We are, as the old saying goes, two nations separated by a common language. You Brits use odd words like *lorry* and *shag*, and no matter how you say them you'll always sound posh to Americans (and have a stiffer upper lip). Despite our differences, however, similarities persist. Indeed, we have our English language. We have our hoary Puritan past. And we have, among other shared cultural predispositions, our enduring love/hate relationship with the French.

Of course you English have a more entrenched history of fighting against the French (and thus, of hating them, passionately), but like countless Americans you continue to be fascinated by them as well. Droves of you seek solace and second homes along the Riviera or the Dordogne. Your own Peter Mayle put Provence on the map, after all, much to the chagrin of every French person living within a hundred kilometer radius of Avignon. British women, like their American sisters, still look at French women as sexy and confounding creatures. And British men, like their American counterparts, cannot think of French women without somehow thinking about love, sex, or both.

Thus, the many references to American culture that dust these pages (I am an American with dual French citizenship) apply to all of us, since we tote the same bag of collective perceptions and clichés about the French. We Anglo-Saxons are sometimes exotic to one another, but we continue to be baffled, seduced, infuriated and enchanted by the Gauls.

Introduction

The first French woman I met in America was an enigmatic neighbor who moved into the Los Angeles enclave where I lived as a girl. This woman was clearly not . . . *normal*. She wore scarves in the sun. She walked the aisles of our local grocery store in cruel-looking high heels, examining produce as if she might perform angioplastic heart surgery on a tomato. Her two kids, pale and well-behaved, wore socks with sandals (a crime in Los Angeles), and they all spoke in forked tongues. In the shaggy-haired aesthetic of Southern California, this woman, whose complicated bun looked positively theatrical if not slightly menacing, had a truly alien quality about her; even her car looked otherworldly. (It was, it turns out, a Citroën DS Cabriolet.) One day, feeling unusually brazen, I approached her in the supermarket while she was analyzing the molecular infrastructure of a cantaloupe and asked where she was from. In one of those harbinger moments she looked back at me and replied: "We're from France."

Ah, so that explained everything. This was years before

the infamous *Saturday Night Live* skit put the Coneheads on our cultural radar, but, in the Happy Face go-go jet age of Los Angeles at that time, it *did* explain her Otherness. Her luxuriant, slightly scary, French-fried Otherness.

Madame France, as I used to call her, went on to become a neighborly friend of sorts. My mother welcomed her to our street with a plate of homemade chocolate-chip cookies. She returned in kind with a bottle of Armagnac. There was the question of the husband—where was he? Was she a widow? A divorcée? No one knew, which only made her more enigmatic. I ended up playing with her two kids, who were petulant and friendly in equal doses, and I recall using my first few lines of French on her and being corrected the time I told her that I was going to eat my dinner. *"Je vais manger mon dîner,"* I said. She shook her head and replied, "No, my dear, animals *eat*. Human beings *dine*." The sheer French velocity of her reply made my knees ache.

At the time, I knew that France was a place of sensual and cultural refuge. Josephine Baker became a star there wearing nothing but pearls and a banana skirt. Henry Miller penned nasty novels in his Parisian "black lace laboratory," which were banned in America. People always flocked to France for intellectual freedom, hot sex, high culture, and fabulous food—not necessarily in that order. And in the firmament of all this, no star shined brighter, it seemed, than the French woman.

The French woman, of course, has enjoyed an alluring and slightly tarty reputation for centuries. She's a coquette, a femme fatale, a sex kitten, a vamp, and a bitch. She's a sophisticate, a fashion hound, an iconoclast, and a rebel. Even her language has remarkably seductive attributes. "Tish! When you speak French, it drives me wild, *cara mia!*" Gomez famously declares to Morticia in *The Addams Family*. (Apparently, her French did wonders for his sinus condition as well.) Ever since the French gave us our Statue of Liberty, they have peppered our culture with their peculiar and piquant ways, enduring as paragons of otherness and dubious stereotypes. The bad guy is often French. The mistress is always French. The bitch and the bastard are usually French (and, while we're at it, the cook, the thief, his wife and her lover). The scary woman with legs out to here is invariably French. And the devil always has a French accent.

No wonder we perceive the French woman as slightly wicked. Her passions are our provocations. We love her and we hate her because she seems to be everything we're not, and because her way of being contradicts our cultural judgments and moral prejudices about love and sex. Plus, we're sure that she's got secrets. It seems she grew up steeped in sensuality while we were raised on canned heat. She certainly seems to know more about giving and receiving pleasure, which means that she's probably having more guilt-free sex than we are and eating a lot more pastry, too.

Like many Americans, I first traveled to France as a student backpacker. A few years later I returned, enrolled myself in the Sorbonne, and moved into a converted broom closet in the posh but gloomy 16th arrondissement with a roommate named Solange.

Solange was from Alsace. She was pale with straw-colored hair and reminded me of a garden elf. Despite this cherubic quality, she had a severity about her that evoked the rustic plains of her ancestral Northern Europe—at least that's how I perceived her penchant for frugality. She ate cheese to the rind, then dried it and grated it into her soup. (Similar rituals were performed with dried half-eaten baguettes.) She was reserved, rarely gesticulated, and had three articles of clothing that she wore over and over again, with tiny adjustments to each look. In short, though Solange was no va-va-voom French girl, she did, despite her curiosities, have a certain undeniable charm and sex appeal, and I recall thinking that if she were a typical French girl, I'd have to adjust my cultural assumptions. I was already aware that the proverbial je ne sais quoi we Anglo-Saxons associate with French women did not have as much to do with surface detail as one might surmise.

During my *séjour* at the Sorbonne I read many *nouveaux romans*, wore many scarves, and through my daily encounters with the natives nurtured my own vigorous love/hate relationship with the French. A thick, delicious year passed, and upon my return to California I assumed that my French days were over.

They were not.

Years later, I met a man working on a film in Los Angeles. I immediately knew that he was French because he was eating a hamburger with a fork. We courted and I moved back to France again, where I married, had two children, and continued to study the local flora and fauna up close. This time I lived in the northeastern fringe of the city's Right Bank, in the 19th arrondissement—a raggedy but rapidly gentrifying working-class swatch of northeastern Paris that I call "Peoples Paris" for the sheer density of humanity packed into it from every corner of the world. (A Parisian friend of mine once sniffed: "I need a passport to enter your neighborhood." At the time, his incurable snobbism deeply impressed me.) It's certainly a reminder that if France is the Eiffel Tower, it's also the Tower of Babel, and that goes for everything beyond the dense supernova of the city's capital as well.

Be that as it may, when I first moved to the 19th you couldn't find it on the maps of many guidebooks. It seemed as if their guidebook writers had laid a cookie cutter on the center of Paris, trimmed off the edges, and discarded them. Only a few landmarks scattered in these northern fringes were mentioned—the Père Lachaise cemetery; Montmartre. Otherwise the only "real" Paris that seemed to exist to purveyors of all things French was its center—namely, the Left Bank.

I bring this up to make a point, which is this: most of the enduring stereotypes we nurture about French women are exported from this center, where so many cultural scribes and tourists stake their claim. It's through the prism of this gilded old hub, in arrondissements nestled around the Seine, that we find our most enduring French cliché. You know her: she's *la Parisienne*, that slightly haughty Frenchie with no body fat, who strolls down boulevard Saint Germain, looking *très chic* and who embodies the word "sexy" like no other. (Disclaimer: I use the word "sexy" throughout this book, well aware that it is among the most overused words on the planet. Hackneyed, blitzed out, postcoital, and postmodern—"sexy" is exhausted by the truly polymorphously perverse weight of its own significance.)

The Left Bank *Parisienne*, however, is not representative of all French women any more than Paris represents all of France, and you don't have to visit the country's ninety-five departments to get wind of this. Just leave the beaten path of the city's center, more a testimony to the city's glorious past than to its polychromatic present, and you'll find plenty of French women who defy the stereotype. And herein lies the challenge of a book of this nature: for every French woman who approaches the stereotype we know so well, there is one who veers dramatically in the other direction; for every Parisienne who looks like she stepped out of *Elle* magazine, clicking her way down the rue de Grenelle in a miniskirt the size of a dinner napkin with the latest Houellebecq novel tucked in her purse, there is another French woman who lives in Saint-Bonnet-le-Château, buys floral print dresses from La Redoute catalog, plays *pétanque* on weekends after she's done singing in her church choir— and *does* get fat.

I'm reminded of the offscreen female narrator in Jean-Luc Godard's 1966 film classic *Masculin, Féminin*. As we watch ordinary French women at work in grainy, black-and-white images, she muses:

> Today in Paris. What do young women dream about? But which young women? The assembly-line inspectors with no time to make love because they're so worn out? The manicurists on the Champs-Elysées who start hooking at age eighteen at the big Right Bank hotels? The rich schoolgirls who only know Bergson and Sartre because their bourgeois parents keep them locked up? There is no average French woman.

No. There is no average French woman, just as there is no average American woman, or Japanese woman, or Italian woman.

And yet.

And yet there she is. The other day I overheard an American man telling a colleague about his boss's new girlfriend. "She's French," was all he said, because that said it all. His colleague raised an eyebrow with a complicitous smile and replied, "Ooh-la-la."

A similar exchange between two American women about somebody's new girlfriend might go something like this:

"She's French."

"Uh-oh."

And that's because no matter what they look like, so many French women still seem to have a luminous sensuality about them. They still seem to be such a . . . menace.

In this creamy mix of Frenchiness—between the bourgeois and the bohemian, the urbanite and the suburbanite—certain French archetypes do indeed prevail, because French culture itself prevails as an infinitely complex web of long-standing rituals and social biases that shapes its citizens. Thus, every day at roughly the same hour, you can still hear the collective scraping of millions of chairs as the French stop the world and sit down en masse to dine at roughly the same hour. They also strike en masse for their common causes, take long vacations with the same summer abandon, read Proust in the metro, cook from scratch, have a keen sense of aesthetics, seek pleasure whenever possible, reject much of the moral dogma that ties us Anglos in knots, and basically prefer having a life over making a living. In short, French culture still turns out puff pastries like it did hundreds of years ago, just as, if we may be gastronomically audacious in our metaphors, it still turns out French women. Which is why there is great truth in what actress Charlotte Rampling once said: "French women have been made beautiful by French people. They're very aware of their bodies, the way they move and speak; they are very confident of their sexuality. French culture has made them like that."

Indeed French culture *has* made them "like that," which is different "from us." And while this difference is at the heart of our fascination with French women, it also makes it impossible to escape the pitfalls of comparing and contrasting cultures—a dicey exercise that runs the risk of exalting French women and, by default, dissing American or British women. Admittedly, my focus is on the most redeeming qualities of these creatures, but the exercise here is not to glorify or ennoble them; rather, it is, as Descartes implied, to contrast cultural values in the hopes that we might see our own in a new light.

Which poses something of a conundrum: England notwithstanding, how can I compare my relatively young culture with its Puritan roots and its extreme attitudes about love and sex to a two-thousand-year-old European culture with infinite layers of sexual and political intrigue and an enduring preoccupation with the pursuit of pleasure? What we have is an apples-and-oranges problem, but that doesn't mean we can't make an interesting fruit salad.

Extreme Frenchness goes back centuries, and this is no history book. That said, at the risk of being profanely abbreviated, let's briefly tip our hat to the centuries that brought us courtly love. From Andreas Capellanus, one of those French guys about whom we know almost nothing but whose prose has the half-life of plutonium, we have this definition of courtly love written in 1184: *"It is the pure love which binds together the hearts of two lovers with every feeling of delight. This kind consists in the contemplation of the mind and the affection of the heart; it goes as far as the kiss and the embrace and the modest*

contact with the nude lover, omitting the final solace, for that is
not permitted for those who wish to love purely. . . . That is called
mixed love which gets its effect from every delight of the flesh and
culminates in the final act of Venus."

Not that the "final act of Venus" didn't preoccupy our
troubadour friends and just about everyone who followed in
their footsteps. Along came the sixteenth century and, with
it, Rabelais, who was so delightfully debauched he enjoys his
own adjective. If "nature abhors a vacuum," as he was fond of
suggesting, then nature must fill every hole. This problem
was one of Rabelais' favorite subjects, and in his seminal
Gargantua and Pantagruel he offers several ways that "the fer-
vency of lust" is abated: drink, drugs, hard labor, and intense
study help counteract the "ardor of lechery" and the inflation
of "the cavernous nerve whose office is to ejaculate the mois-
ture for the propagation of human progeny."

Other libertines followed Rabelais and lubricated French
society with their scandalous ruminations (infamous sex
junkie Marquis de Sade immediately comes to mind), but
Rabelais stands out in my mind for his sense of humor. If
there's one thing that he taught the French and that seems to
have stuck over the centuries, it's that sex is funny. It is also
tragic, strange, rhapsodic, and deliciously poignant. But it
is often funny. And if you don't have a sense of humor about
sex, it only stands to reason that you might not have much fun
having sex in the first place. Put this Rabelaisian attitude in
your shaker along with the romantic spirit of courtly love, add

a dash of gravitas *and* frivolity, and you get a cocktail that still infuses French women and sets them apart from their Anglo sisters.

Nowhere do we Anglos differ more dramatically than when it comes to attitudes about love and sex. In 1833, Ralph Waldo Emerson summed up what still remains a truth for many today when he wrote in his diary: "Young men are very fond of Paris, partly, no doubt, because of the perfect freedom—freedom from observation as well as interferences—in which each one walks after the sight of his own eyes." Getting more to the point about why such perfect freedom might be Absolutely Fabulous, Washington Irving wrote that French women were "admirably calculated to set fire to the head and set fire to the tail." Given that men's heads are often in their tails, the arrangement worked brilliantly.

It may be a long historical jump in time between then and now, but it's a short leap in social consciousness when it comes to the enduring misperceptions we Anglos still carry around in our heads about the French. If we continue to revere them when it comes to their savoir faire in matters of the heart (that is, when we're not reviling them), it's because we know that many of our hang-ups don't exist in France. We know that in France we have permission to leave our puritanical baggage at the door—to lighten the load. We know that the French generally understand how to make love, not war, while we're still stuck with border skirmishes in an ongoing battle of the sexes.

Indeed, love and sex are doing just fine in France, *merci beaucoup*. For a bit of hard-core data in that department, say *bonjour* to Janine Mossuz-Lavau, one of those deeply attractive French women of "a certain age" who also happens to be the director of research at CNRS (Centre National de la Recherche Scientifique) and the author most recently of *La Vie Sexuelle en France*. If you don't have the time to read 421 pages of dense French research, we'll bottom-line it for you: "The sex and love life of 'real [French] people' is vibrant, tragic, and funny at the same time," Mossuz-Lavau writes. Or as the French newsmagazine *L'Express* happily summed it up in reviewing her book: "In France there is an art of love that is being cultivated that is at once serious and lighthearted, tender and demanding. A tranquil form of hedonism."

A tranquil form of hedonism—sounds dreamy at a time when sex sells everything, but love remains as elusive as ever. If there's one thing that French women seem to know in all this delectation, it's that love and sex rarely conform to predetermined strategies, how-to ground rules, or dating dogma. As they'll often tell you without much hesitation, finding happy trails in love and sex often involves trekking into Terra Incognita without a compass, but with a resolute openness to experiencing life in all its ravishing complexity. Which leads us back through the centuries to Madame de Scudéry.

Madame de Scudéry was a prominent member of seventeenth-century literary high life in Paris. Between the years of 1654 and 1661 she wrote and published a novel called *Clélie*. It featured an allegorical Map of Love ("La Carte du Tendre"—the Map of Tenderness), which depicted the vicissitudes of love and the geography of the heart. While it might have seemed campy in its time (French poet Boileau satirized it in his book *Les héros de roman*), it nonetheless had its moment of glory, illustrating how French women were concerned with even the most pedestrian matters of love and sex centuries ago.

The departure point on the Map of Love is a familiar town called New Friendship (located, appropriately enough, at the bottom of the map). The landscape is traversed by three great rivers—Esteem, Recognition, and Inclination—and is surrounded by various bodies of water (the Lake of Indifference, the Sea of Intimacy, and the Sea of Danger). Scattered about are habitats more or less favorable to love: there are Villages of Tenderness, Negligence, and Generosity; Towns of Probity, Respect, Sincerity, and Passion; and Hamlets of Submission, Diligence, and even Grooming Habits. All roads, however, lead not to Rome but toward that deeply appealing and ultimately perilous place called "Unknown Lands." Wrote Madame de Scudéry: "The River of Inclination empties into what we call the Sea of Danger; and then beyond this Sea we find what we call Unknown Lands, because in fact we know not what lies ahead."

Centuries later, her words are still relevant. The landscape

- - - - - - - - -

of the heart is universal and timeless, the Unknown continues to sweep its way through the peaks and valleys of amorous
encounters, and French women still remain—despite themselves and the clichés thrown at their feet—paragons of a life
more fully and freely lived.

One

MEN

On loving men "a lot, a lot," the "F" word, gender friskiness, why a man is not an emu, fiercely French wardrobe malfunctions, the commingling of contradictions, and the beauty of living in the middle ground

We want the power to seduce and be seduced. There will never be a war of the sexes in France.

—FRENCH FEMINIST
SYLVIANE AGACINSKI

Under a king, a country is really ruled by a woman.

—LOUIS XIV OF FRANCE

Not long ago I attended a dinner party in Paris and sat among a group of French women who all looked like they'd just engaged in illicit and terribly wonderful things with their partners. Wineglasses clinked as they laughed, threw back their heads, and talked about men. They were not commiserating about men—no whiff of disgruntlement or free-floating frustration filled the air. This was no familiar bitch session. Rather, as hands flew deftly about the table, they all seemed to share a love and abiding appreciation for members of the opposite sex.

Take note, dear reader, that there is no popular vernacular expression in French for "the opposite sex" that bears the same weight as in English. The Anglo-Saxon term literally translates into a clinical epithet that sounds somewhat warlike, and if you use it too staunchly, French women will think you are speaking of a spider monkey or some other dangerous primate. Men are not "opposite" as in a "species" or a "phylum," which is not to say that they are anything at all like us.

- - - - - - - - - -

Au contraire. These French women seemed to understand this distinction in a fundamental way. They had secret knowledge about men that was both carnal and cerebral. They were Spies in the House of Love.

Fans of French erotica might be reminded of Anaïs Nin's novella of the same name right about now. That said, as I fumbled at the table (personally I was interested in a bitch session), it was Marguerite Duras, that grande dame of twentieth-century letters, who came to mind: "You have to love men a lot," she once wrote. "A lot, a lot. You have to love men a lot. Otherwise they are simply unbearable."

Readers, let us bite into the Big Camembert with this: In France men and women actually like one another. A lot. There is no Anglo-style war of the sexes going on. French men and women actually want to be together. They enjoy their mutual company. They spar. They debate. They flirt. They seek out one another's company in a multiplicity of social settings. Anyone who's dined with the French will be struck by the boy-girl-boy-girl seating arrangements imposed by the host or hostess. This is more than simply stuffy protocol, of which the French are, of course, connoisseurs.

Witness the first French dinner party I attended. I was seated by our hostess, Claudine, an austere film editor from Brittany. She stood by her table with that trademark pout for which French women are famous the world over (it was one of those long wooden tables, by the way, that are authentically distressed because they've actually been *used* for decades), and assessed each guest with a critical eye to determine who should sit where. *"You will sit . . . here, Jean-Claude, and you . . . mais non! Paulette, wait, you must go there . . . and you, Dominique, you should go here, and. . . ."*

The bottom line: Women were not to sit in henlike clusters. Men were not to chum in packs. Spouses were denied the comfort of familiarity and were separated at opposite ends of the table. The point of this exercise was to achieve the juiciest, most well-balanced gender* diversity at her table, because according to the simple laws that foster complicity among the French, conversation (not to mention, life in general) is far more interesting when the sexes intermix—when intellectual friskiness, innocent flirtations, tête-à-têtes, and other forms of spontaneous combustion are encouraged.

At the time, Claudine's seating machinations seemed a little forced and old-fashioned to me (those were the days when slicing a wedge from a foot-high cone of goat cheese without slicing into the plate was enough to send me into a panic), and as she steered everyone to their seats with a slightly stern directive, I thought: What's next, name tags? Must everything be so ritualized? Would I figure out the cutlery? And did I *have* to sit next to a man who smoked hand-rolled

---

*A word about gender: The word "gender" in French translates into the rather fuzzy and ambivalent word "genre." It has neither the clinical precision nor punch of the English word, suggesting a sexual neutrality the French do not find particularly compelling. Additionally, "gender studies" exists primarily in rarefied university circles in France, which is why if you mention the subject, most ordinary French people will look at you as if you were trying to explain the mating habits of an exotic tetrapod.

cigarettes the size of bread sticks and looked like Sartre with better hair?

After the first round of drinks was polished off and glasses ceremoniously refilled, a few questions were thrown obliquely my way from dinner guests hotly debating the Clinton/Lewinsky scandal (those were the days. . . .). Why did this political "fellationship" so fascinate my fellow Americans? I was asked. How could such a shallow but common act preoccupy a nation? What was wrong with Americans? To which I could only respond, once the battered subject of puritanism had been laid out on its stretcher, *Je ne sais pas*. I did learn that night, however, that we owe the Western world's first literary blow job to Rabelais, that those things that look like surgical tweezers for extracting nose hairs are in fact for snails, and that snails are far more appetizing when you call them escargots.

Sartre turned out to be a charming clarinetist, who helped me slice into that foot-high cone of chèvre while quoting a line attributed to French gastronomist Jean Anthelme Brillat-Savarin that was so odd I instantly adored the man: "A dinner which ends without cheese," he said," is like a beautiful woman with only one eye."

Meanwhile, the wife whose husband was nestled between two women at the far end of the table spent the evening enjoying the constant attention of another male guest; and her husband, who stole occasional glances over the tops of a now stunning array of empty Pomerol bottles, seemed genuinely amused to see his wife become the discreet object of desire of another man.

If French men don't take offense when their wives attract the admiration of other men (*au contraire*, the thought that their wives still have a seductive edge is often a source of pride, as annoyingly continental as that may sound), French women also relish these seductive flirtations rather than rebuff them. In fact, they expect them. They participate in them. Dare I say they even feel that life is bereft without them? Because flirtation is alive and well in France, *merci beaucoup*. It is a civic duty. It is the French drug of choice. It is the lifeblood that beats at the core of French society. Young women flirt. Older women flirt. Even feminists flirt.

"Did I really set out to do my best to charm you?" French feminist Françoise Giroud once asked Bernard-Henri Lévy in a smart if not abstruse little book called *Women and Men: A Philosophical Conversation*, "I'm sure I must have done it spontaneously, because you were a good-looking, dynamic young man and it amused me to catch your attention. But for what purpose? For nothing. For a moment of pleasure, the pleasure of being able, fleetingly, to charm another person. I must confess I've enjoyed that pleasure my whole life."

Now a flirtatious feminist might be an oxymoron in America (I can already hear spears rustling in the forest), but in France you will see this creature everywhere with her iron fist in her velvet glove. Though France has always been the land of love, let's not forget that it has also always been the land of sexism. That said, French women never danced on the hot coals of American-style feminism; their feminism burned with less militancy and lacked, as French historian Mona Ozouf saw it, the "unparalleled dimensions and unprecedented ferocity" of its Anglo counterpart. Put in racier terms, journalist Justine De Lacy pointed out in *The New York Times* during feminism's heyday that "French women, after all, did not exactly remove veils upon liberation; many did remove bras, but this was more in celebration than in protest against the female condition."

Precisely. And so it's come to pass (a turn of phrase that prunes away decades of complicated suffragette culture we simply can't squeeze into these pages) that enjoying the perks of femininity does not implicate French women in a plot to sustain their inadequacy, any more than sharing a deep complicity with men implies an abandonment of power. On the contrary, it tends to imbue them with a particular strength and commonsense wisdom about men that's been obscured in the Sturm und Drang of our gender-conflicted times.

You can take a $500 lifestyle workshop in America to get wind of this, or you can have a drink with a French woman. Here's what she'll tell you: a man is not a woman (or an emu, but we'll get to that). He cannot think like you. He cannot "process" like you. When it comes to the game of love, he will not rise to the plate with the same meticulous and urgent sensibility as you do. In fact, as we'll explore in pages to come, the only thing that will rise up if you push him too hard to emote like you will be the hair on his back, even if he has none to speak of. Other parts of his anatomy will not respond with quite the same vertical lift. Somewhere in our heart of hearts we know this. We've learned that men are from Mars and we're from Venus and we're all stuck in intergalactic gridlock, but that hasn't stopped us from trying hard to neutralize the differences between men and women and level the playing field. That said, men can't wear high-impact sports bras any more than we can wear jockstraps. At least, not without feeling ridiculous.

In short, when it comes to personal relationships, French women often prefer to play the field rather than level it. They accept with a certain fatalism the contradictions and imperfections of men—their insolences and their extravagances; their pigheadedness and their seductions. They understand, or at least find intriguing, the emotional grottoes where men often retreat like bears. "Men, in their silence, are moving," French actress and director Nicole Garcia once opined. "They shut themselves up, they don't ask for anything, they just want us to leave them alone. They don't have the same confidence that we do in speaking, in analyzing emotion with words. . . . They reveal who they are more through their actions, and it's in that moment that I want to understand them, to break through their mystery."

This "mystery," to hit you over the head with this point like a frying pan (preferably a Le Creuset), is all wrapped up in negotiating and playing with *la différence* between men and women. It's predicated on a certain passion for men, if not an actual compassion for them, which might seem desperately hoary and 1950s in its compliant acknowledgment of gender differences (me, Tarzan; you, Jane). But let's recall that the scent of a woman who loves men is a strong one indeed, and in this culture of male/female complicity, that's one heady draw, no matter what you look like. In Bertrand Blier's film *Too Beautiful for You*, Bernard (Gérard Depardieu) is married to bombshell beauty Florence (Chanel model Carole Bouquet) but falls passionately in love with his slightly frumpy secretary, in part because her swooning delight in his manhood is an irresistible seduction compared with his beautiful but emotionally glacial trophy wife. ("What's left to desire when you have perfection?" Bernard asks his wife at one point. The answer: Not much.)

Because this gender friskiness has such deep historical roots, French women not only enjoy flirtation, they expect it. "If I spend a lot of time with a man and he doesn't flirt in even a casual or playful way, I'm actually somewhat offended," my friend Sophie once said. The hint of sexuality that infuses flirtation is not perceived as a threat; on the contrary, it's perceived as a necessary and even ordinary expression of difference: the way negative and positive make a charge; the way a male plug fits into a female socket (the world of power tools just brims with high-voltage metaphors). To quote Alain Giami, research director at INSERM (Institut National de la Santé et de la Recherche Médicale), coauthor of a sprawling comparative Franco-American sex study, and a multipurpose analyst of the human libido, "The French do not consider flirtation and seduction as a direct sexual approach, and flirtation does not necessarily lead to intercourse." How reassuring. With a juicier take on the same subject, French writer and social critic Elisabeth Weissman describes flirtation as simply "the promise of *coït* that is communicated between men and women, even if it never happens."

That's the *promise* of *coït*, not the threat of it.

That French women enjoy this "promise" as a seductive tease that lingers, unconsummated, in their brushes with strangers and chance encounters with ordinary men— that they might appreciate flirtation the way they appreciate éclairs lined up like so many tiny pastel ballerinas waiting to be eaten at their local *boulangerie* (to be approached with pleasure *and* restraint, in other words)—says more about the difference between us and them than all your sociology textbooks combined. That Anglo women are able to let their hair down in France and enjoy the spark of that promise is also a tribute to French culture itself. Take this post from the blog Polly-Vous Francais:

"Last month at the *Carrefour* at Auteuil, in the checkout lane for home delivery, in front of me was a tall, ruggedly handsome man, clearly just back from vacation. He was wearing Bermudas and Top-Siders, a polo shirt and a great tan. Tousled hair. I was doing my own 'checkout' by trying to determine his domestic status (and) analyzing what he was buying. . . . Anyway, I did eventually notice a wedding ring on his finger, so he was off-limits, officially, at any rate. However, when it was my turn . . . the clerk said, 'What else can we do for you, madame? *Vous êtes avec le monsieur, n'est-ce pas?*' (You are with the gentleman, correct?)

I replied, with my best stage sigh and engaging smile, '*Non, hélas!*'

Mr. Tousled Hair was flattered and amused, and gave me a glittering glance and complicitous nod as he headed out the door.

It was a great little moment of connecting. (I would NEVER have done that in puritanical Massachusetts, especially not as a divorced woman. Bad, bad, bad.) I guess part of it is that in France it feels as though it's your duty to show appreciation of beauty or something pleasing."

Indeed it *is* your duty to show appreciation of beauty or something pleasing in France; it is also your duty to enjoy the "promise of *coït*" even if it never happens (not that you'd ever want it to happen, right?). This is not bad, bad, bad. *Non, non, non.* In fact it is so good, good, good that Weissman credits flirtation as having saved gender relations in France "at a time when men risk being emasculated by women."

- - - - - - - - -

Because French women live and love in this mental geography of a boy-girl-boy-girl world—and because they still manage to keep the *femme* in feminism, as terribly flippant as that may sound (more spears clattering in the forest here)—they're less inclined to expect the kind of gender egalitarianism that Anglo women tend to seek out in relationships. French women have other ways of tacking their sails against the gales in these choppy waters.

"Strict egalitarianism, with its punitive overtones, doesn't work," says Fabienne Casta-Rosaz, French author of *Histoire du Flirt* and *Histoire de la sexualité en Occident*. "It's not equality that counts, it's reciprocity that counts. I might pick up after my companion or do the laundry, but I won't necessarily expect him to take out the trash or do something that has the same weight." My friend Cécile puts it this way: "Love is not like a balance sheet. There's no such thing as double-entry accounting when it comes to love. 'I did this for you; now you do that.' Love and sex don't work that way. It's not about tit for tat. It's not like you're trading one pound of cheese for two kilos of walnuts. Living happily with men is about finding a way to achieve reciprocity and complementarity, not perfect fifty-fifty egalitarianism."

That sounded so simple it was almost dumbfounding, like the chaos theory of the universe or $E = mc^2$. But if French women are like those Spies in the House of Love, it's partly thanks to this interpretation of gender differences. Likewise, if Anglo women seem to exist somewhere on the opposite side

----

of the spectrum, it's due to a very different experience of the same thing. And herein lies the root of various "confusions of love," to quote French therapist Danièle Flaumenbaum, which have a particularly American flavor to them.

The evolutionary scale is long and densely inhabited with these "confusions." Writer Caitlin Flanagan, who writes frequently on modern mommydom, picked away at some of these "confusions" when she suggested that while marriage used to provide access to sex, it now provides access to celibacy, partly because women are endlessly frustrated by men's incapacity to meet them halfway in the drudgery of domestic life. Writes Flanagan: "women are left with two options: endlessly haranguing their husbands to be more womanly, or silently fuming and (however wittingly) launching a sex strike of an intensity and a duration that would have impressed Aristophanes. The men who cave in to the pressure to become more feminine—putting little notes in the lunch boxes, sweeping up after snack time, the whole bit—may delight their wives, but they probably don't improve their sex lives much, owing to the thorny old problem of *la différence*."

Merci, Madame Flanagan, for referring to the French term here. Because French women are more culturally inclined to embrace *la différence*, they generally don't engage in "sex strikes" and the strain to make men "become more feminine" in the first place. The jury is out as well on whether they think treating your man like a house pet or an exotic animal works any better. In "What Shamu Taught Me About a Happy Marriage," Amy Sutherland described in *The New York Times* how she applied exotic animal training techniques to her husband, with great success. These techniques involved acknowledging good behavior and ignoring bad behavior (equally practical on small infants!). "I used to take his faults personally; his dirty clothes on the floor were an affront, a symbol of how he didn't care enough about me," she wrote. "But thinking of my husband as an exotic species gave me the distance I needed to consider our differences more objectively."

Subtly spoofed in French *Elle*, this notion might sound delightfully zoomorphic; still, it makes you wonder: Must we compare men to wild hedgehogs or mud snails, to understand that they're different from us? We can't "fix" an emu and turn it into a horse, any more than we can "fix" a man and turn him into a woman. I'm reminded of Barbra Streisand, who once asked, "Why does a woman work ten years to change a man's habits and then complain that he's not the man she married?" Albert Einstein put it differently: "Men marry women with the hope they will never change. Women marry men with the hope they will change. Invariably they are both disappointed." Smart guy. When we Anglo women aren't busy trying to change ourselves, we're often busy trying to change our men. A recent feature in an American women's magazine titled "Can You Fix Him?" drove this point home. "Instead of shoring up our slumping husbands, we're *showing* them up," the article explained. Maybe, the article concludes, it's time to consider a more benevolent, Zen-like, and realistic view about men. For expediency's sake, I'll sum up that view in one handy proverb: you can't change human nature but you *can* attract more bees with honey.

Bonjour. French women seem to have known this annoying little platitude for centuries. As Marie put it: "Men are like puppies. Screaming doesn't work. If you annoy them too much, they bite. If you upstage them, they'll go in their caves. If the leash is too tight, they will try to run free. If you use your emotional intelligence in more subtle ways, your man will eventually follow you like a springer spaniel. And if he doesn't, then you are probably really with the wrong guy."

This sounded so retro when I first heard it that my inner feminist nearly gagged, but Marie had a point. Why fight when you can finesse? Why try to modify your mate's behavior when this classic but futile exercise generally entrenches one more firmly in the no-fly zone of domestic ennui? Why endlessly try to reinvent, cajole, destroy, rebuild, or otherwise fix what might not be broken? These are fine and noble traits if you're building a transcontinental railway or sending global positioning satellites into space; a little more problematic when you're building relationships with imperfect, and often perplexing, sentient beings called men.

One remedy for this comes our way from French author Véronique Vienne, who offers this simple nugget: "Make peace with the fact that some of the best people in your life

----

are fallible, unreasonable, and downright annoying." This, of course, implies making peace with a different way of making peace. I'm reminded of that scene in *My Big Fat Greek Wedding*, when our heroine's mother manages to convince her husband to agree to something she wants by making him think it's *his* idea. "Men may be the head of the house," the mother says, "but the women are the neck, and they can turn the head any way they want."

Okay, she was Greek, but never mind. French women do have a way of asserting the power of being a woman without necessarily going to war like a man, and of negotiating *la différence* on the front line of love and sex rather than striving for what French novelist Camille Laurens once lamented as "the fake abolition of otherness that makes everyone so uniform and falsely familiar." Their headspace is less cloudy with the desire to fix and rewire the immutable vagaries of their mates; nor is it filled with the moral menace of the Politically Correct (though they *will* throw you in etiquette prison for using the wrong cheese knife).

ONE DAY, SHORTLY AFTER my return to the States, I was listening to the radio with my son and stumbled on shock jock Tom Leykis. At the time, Leykis was to misogyny what Howard Stern is to sex, and that day he was on a roll: "Prepare to breed another generation of pussy-whipped males who have to pee sitting down!" he screamed into the mike. I sat there, listening with my mouth open, until my son asked, "Mommy, what's *pussy-whipped*?"

Now the only thing more difficult than explaining the term to a five-year-old is trying to translate it into French. There's the expression "*dominé par sa femme*" [literally translated, "a man who is dominated by his woman"—not quite the same punch to *that* term] or the harmless "*C'est la femme qui porte les culottes*," or "It's the woman who wears the pants." No pussies or whips or even chain saws in sight, partly because the vitriol simmering here isn't mainlined into French culture the way it is in America. Listening to Leykis vent his spleen to American men, I couldn't help but recall that nearly fifteen years earlier, poet Robert Bly had asked American men to get in touch with their inner male by camping in forests and beating on drums. Now Leykis was asking them to do much the same thing by getting mad, getting laid, and getting even with women ["*Pump 'em and dump 'em!*"]. American men had gone from drum-beating to chest-beating in barely a decade, and it couldn't bode well for love or sex. That said, when Leykis yelled into his mike, "All of my boys [his listeners] have gotten their hearts carved out by women!" one couldn't help but wonder: Deep down, do these guys really want to get laid, or get loved?

This question would be rhetorical to French men. They want to get loved *and* get laid, but not because they have an ax to grind against women. Rather, it's because, like French women, they also tend to love the opposite sex *a lot, a lot*. Thus, when American-style sociofeminist questions pop up in France (and nearly everything American pops up there like so many fusty mushrooms), the answers are undeniably, well, French. "Can we exalt the differences between the sexes without being accused of plotting against egalitarianism?" Weissman asks in a special issue of French *Elle*. Gatekeepers of high culture—men and women—chime in with a resounding *oui*. Camille Laurens, whose entire literary oeuvre is dedicated to the hot and hairy geography of the opposite sex, goes further, raising her hat to "that beautiful organ that nature has bestowed upon men." Weissman joins in on the toast, enthusing: "Blessed be the penis, that undeniable physical difference that allows both sexes to fit so snugly together."

Blessed be the penis? That beautiful organ? Dorothy, I have a feeling we're not in Kansas anymore.

Before we click our red slippers and go home, let's recall that French women have pushed their pens on behalf of "that beautiful organ" for quite some time. One need only crack open the sometimes campy debauchery in Anaïs Nin's *Delta of Venus*, or read Pauline Réage's *Story of O* or Emmanuelle Arsan's *Emmanuelle* (the latter two of which were written when America was still in bobby socks). More contemporary and existentially tormented male anatomy salutes us in the work of French filmmaker Catherine Breillat, who brought the first jumbo-size penis to mainstream cinema in her controversial movie *Romance*. Then, there are the many perversely and pathologically probing penises in Catherine Millet's *The Sexual Life of Catherine M.* My favorite, however, is the more pensive penis that comes our way in Véronique Vienne's latest book, *The Art of Being a Woman*.

According to Vienne, the penis is perceptive. "When a penis figures out that you are in a receptive mood, it wants to prance, frolic, and romp," writes Vienne. This same penis, however, "is going to sulk when it finds out that you feel fat and ugly, that you are upset about your new haircut, or that you are worried about what you are going to wear at your sister's wedding." A divining rod of sorts, the penis "can tell when you are genuinely interested in a conversation, when you'd like to be asked to dance, when you think it would be nice to be kissed, or when you wish the evening would never end." Presumably, this same penis can also tell when you'd like it to stop dancing and finish cleaning out the garage. If there's such a thing as a Thinking Woman's Penis, it would have to be French.

Now, I don't know about you, but I can't recall the last time I saw an homage to male anatomy in any mainstream American women's venue. Vaginas might have their monologues, but penises? Frankly, in the reigning dogma of our American times, men are still from Mars and their penises are a big part of the problem. In fact, it seems we not only don't want them prancing around too energetically, we don't even want those penises going on vacation with us. Not long ago my husband noticed an American ad for a mainstream cruise line selling

- - - - - - - - -

Ladies Only cruises that featured a photo of women beaming together in what looked like a tropical paradise. I don't recall the headline, but I do remember my husband asking of the ad: "Are those women *happy* gay . . . or *gay* gay?" It hardly seemed to matter. The point was that men were out of the picture and these women were overjoyed about it.

Indeed female-bonding industries are blooming all over the country, catering to the desire to keep men out of our hair—and provide welcome relief in the process. "I'd rather spend the evening with my rabbit than go out and deal with men," says Charlotte York in an episode of *Sex and the City*—and she isn't speaking of a fuzzy bunny. Maureen Dowd's *Are Men Necessary?* says it all in the title alone.

Think about it: by French standards we Anglos do indeed socialize in great same-sex packs. We have our Ladies Nights, our bachelor parties, and our chick nights; we have our bridesmaids and our grooms and even our ex-wives clubs. We have our sororities and our fraternities (which literally don't exist in France and which, once explained to the baffled French, appear medieval with their feuding same-sex fiefdoms). We have such a stunning array of gender-specific clubs, associations, networks, and groups that *O* magazine headlined a recent article on bar-hopping, ladies-only, cocktail-guzzling excesses with the alarming question: ARE GIRLS THE NEW GUYS? Talk about a new spin on gender studies. "At the mirrored bar, six shiny-haired women lean together in ardent conversation," René Steinke reports. "Their blouses are slinky or sheer, their eyes mascaraed and bracelets jangling, not for the men casting glances in their direction but for one another."

Of course French women bond, kick back cocktails, and talk about *les hommes* like the rest of us. But let us understand that because men must be *in* the picture, not out of it, they generally flinch when these relationships become clannish, associative, clubby, or otherwise so exclusive and gender-specific that commiseration about men replaces complicity with them; they chafe when relations between the sexes become so segregated that men are removed from the aesthetic or intellectual equation. No wonder even our beloved *Sex and the City* managed to fluff the fur of a few powerful French felines the wrong way. "What is the most successful and most puritan sitcom of recent years?" asks writer/editor Valérie Toranian in her book *Pour en finir avec la femme*. "*Sex and the City*. These orgasmic and smart single women are perhaps cute and fun but incapable of settling down. They will finish life in their high heels, thin, sad and all alone."

Our infamous *Sex and the City* friends *did* end up shacked by the end of the series—Hollywood loves a Happy Ending, after all. And *Sex and the City* was also a big hit in France. (Then again so was *Baywatch*. Go figure.) But Toranian's point is that in the segregated female urban tribes that populate America, there are not only the enduring seeds of gender warfare that still sprout in our domestic gardens; there is also the not-so-distant effluvia of our puritanical past.

- - - - - - - - -

FRANÇOISE GIROUD ONCE REMARKED that in France, "relations between men and women are and remain the best in the world, even if it isn't always paradise." No, it's not always paradise. French men can be arrogant, macho, and simply "intolerable." There's a reason, after all, why the national mascot is a cock. That said, there's also a reason why the symbol of the Republic is a woman. Reproduced ad infinitum on nearly every piece of national paraphernalia, we know her best as Marianne, the symbol of the French Republic represented in Delacroix's *Liberty Leading the People*: there she is, our Gallic goddess storming the Bastille with bayonet in one hand and French flag in another, her frock unfurled and her bare breasts defiant against the onslaught of enemy fire. All *femme* and fury, Marianne is a true paragon of the French woman: first, she's accessorized (check out that Phrygian bonnet and that braided belt!). Second, she's composed and comfortable in the company of men. Third, she's political and passionate. Fourth, she's topless.

Marianne is an embodiment of a huge range of national virtues, but what *about* those breasts? "The Republic prefers an opulent, more maternal breast, with its promise of generosity and abundance," explains writer/historian Maurice Agulhon, adding that perfectly balanced breasts that are exactly the same size are "an additional symbol of the

egalitarian spirit." The artist Daumier, who called his Marianne "a strong woman with a powerful bosom," depicted the
national goddess topless with two male figures sucking happily at her mountainous breasts. Numerous bosomy rendi-
tions of Marianne followed.

Leave it to the French to embody their national values in the
form of mythic, rebellious women endowed with special virtues:
Joan of Arc heard voices. Marianne had great breasts. No wonder
supermodel Laetitia Casta, who once declared that her breasts
were raised on butter and crème fraîche, was elected the latest
embodiment of Marianne. Of this great honor Casta (who shares
the legacy with Brigitte Bardot and Catherine Deneuve) said:
"To represent France, liberty, and a certain idea of what a woman
is—that's a hell of a responsibility." No kidding.

The first time I saw Delacroix's Marianne, I, too, was
impressed by her flamboyant French breasts, particularly by
the way they led her nation into battle without underwire support. (A recent *New Yorker* cartoon: a mother and her young
son in the Louvre look up at Delacroix's portrait of Marianne.
Mother: "Yes, Johnny, it *is* a wardrobe malfunction.") I tried
to conjure up a similar female icon in the States. The Statue of
Liberty immediately came to mind, but, hey, she was made in
France. The closest I could come up with was the stern pitch-
fork maiden in Grant Wood's *American Gothic*, who, with her
prudish air of joyless utilitarianism, is a far cry from Marianne. Frankly, who would you rather have as your personal
icon and nation's calling card?

- - - - - - - - -

Marianne, I might add, is not alone. French women get Héloïse, who goes back to the Middle Ages and whose love for Abélard was so intense she was willing to ignore social conventions and the religious morality of her time to assert her sexual desires. They got Joan of Arc, with her love not necessarily of men but of the Guy Who Made Them in His Image. Joan heard voices, drove legions into battle, and became a rebel, mystic, warrior, saint, and martyr all by the time she was nineteen. (Now *that* smells like teen spirit.) Lest we forget that, like Joan of Arc, the Patron Saint of Paris, Saint Geneviève was also a French girl of humble origins with speed-dial access to God who prevented Atilla the Hun from sacking Paris, among other amazing feats. And then there's Marianne, who represents the ordinary French girl next door endowed with extraordinary national virtues, including the most famous bosom on the continent. While it might be far-fetched to suggest that the rebellious and iconoclastic spirit of these sovereign figures has insinuated itself into the French woman's gene pool, we'll do it anyhow.

Other mavericks have held their torch high for French women, of course, including the singularly illustrious Simone de Beauvoir, and if there's one thing that they all evoke, it's that particular French mélange of femininity and female force; it's a reminder that despite its inherent sexism, French society still allows women to assume their femininity and their sexuality in a man's world without completely subverting or wildly exaggerating both to placate dominant masculine values. Lucky French women—they grow up with the symbolic virtues of Marianne's fiery femaleness and her unapologetic wardrobe malfunction. They grow up with more cultural permission to claim their sexuality as a birthright and a source of power, which gives them a certain quiet splendor. Where we Anglo women once raised our fists and danced to Helen Reddy's "I Am Woman, Hear Me Roar," French women didn't have to shout quite so loudly about it, in part because as French historian Emmanuel Le Roy Ladurie once put it, "France is, first of all, a woman. A beautiful woman."

FAST-FORWARD TO THE PRESENT. In a *New York Times* essay ("Changing My Feminist Mind, One Man at a Time"), writer J. Courtney Sullivan describes her dating woes as a struggle "with two competing images of the opposite sex: oppressor and dream date." This Beau-and-the-Beast dichotomy is reinforced by her gender studies, which fanned the flames in Sullivan's conflicted heart until she became enraged—"enraged and utterly confused," to be precise. How could she be a feminist and harbor romantic dream-boy fantasies? How could she manage her "rage toward men in general" with the "desire to meet that one specific man who could make my dreams come true"? Was it possible to pursue her "proposed life of egalitarian bliss" while simultaneously loving and hating men?

Eventually, our girl seems to understand that "egalitarian bliss" might be more problematic than she'd bargained for. After several failed relationships she finally finds a guy with whom she can embrace certain contradictions. In short, she "discovers a world between the harsh reality of sexism and the airy wishes of my love-drenched fantasies."

This place between the extremes of militant feminism and romantic fantasy is generally where French women live. It even has a name. It's called *le juste milieu*—or the middle ground. To translate *le juste milieu* as "middle ground" seems sadly unpoetic, but it's the best we can do.

The *juste milieu* is that middle place between the toasty passion of the Latin soul and the frostier outposts of the Cartesian mind. It's a place not colored by the extremes of angry feminist or baby-doll romantic, princess or porn queen. You don't have to burn bras or pad them to live here; rather, you can embody with ease many of the contradictions that we Anglo-Saxon women refute or struggle with: You can be feminine *and* a feminist. A sensualist and a traditionalist. Classic and libertine. Submissive and powerful. Compliant and defiant. Living in that middle ground, you're less polarized by the moral extremes of good/bad and right/wrong, and, for reasons we'll cover in pages to come, you're able to negotiate a world where romantic possibilities don't have to be emotionally tidy or safe. Desire can be of greater import than utility, experience of greater import than resolutions and "closures." Entanglements, flirtations, and liaisons don't necessarily have to be *dangereuses* and can unfold in plotless but appealing provocations made possible thanks to that special thing called gender. French society is far from perfect, but it continues to be a place where, to quote Mona Ozouf, "the demand for equality among individuals remains fundamental, but can be combined with an emphasis on differences. These differences can be experienced without anxiety and can even be used with felicity; people can play on the resources of seduction and the ambiguity of amorous relationships; they can run the infinite gamut of romance." All of which is a way of saying that when French women say *vive la différence*, they really mean it.

AMAZONS AND ANGELS

"Men and women were separated socially in your society," social scientist Alain Giami once elaborated in a phone discussion. "That's a very important historical element that distinguishes Anglo-Saxon culture and French culture. You have much more 'homosociality' in your culture." Let us forgive Giami the unbearably anthropological ring of the word homosociality and consider that he has a point. In fact let's make like the French, for whom the past is sexy and still very much alive, and take that point back a few centuries.

The 1700s were high times for all that gender complicity in France. Literary salons were cultivated by women who were often engaged in common crusades with men, and Power Couples like Madame de Châtelet and Voltaire made headlines in a remarkable alliance of beauty and brains. The atmosphere was hot, heady, political, and filled with innumerable opportunities for *liaisons dangereuses*—and the French liked it that way.

This culture of Extreme Frenchness set a lasting tone in the land of Gaul despite the Revolution (not a good time for love or sex). Back then, Thomas Jefferson took one look at permissive Parisian women and, comparing them to pious American maidens, declared: "A comparison of amazons to angels!" (Too bad he didn't live long enough to meet Britney Spears.)

Jefferson went on to lament vigorously the politically engaged French women who rubbed perhaps more than just elbows with men in high places. "The tender breasts of ladies were not formed for political convulsions," he said, "and the French ladies miscalculate much to their own happiness when they wander from the true field of their influence into that of politicks [*sic*]." Needless to say, French women frowned on this frosty world view. Madame de Staël, whose tender breast did indeed wander into the field

- - - - - - - - - -

of politics, was twenty-three years younger than Jefferson and characterized the segregated same-sex social groups of Jefferson's Anglo-Saxon culture as "chilly enclosures." She felt strongly, as French historian Mona Ozouf writes, that "lost in such a society is the stereophonic richness of the exchange between the sexes."

In different gardens different flowers shall bloom.* One tribute to French feminism is that the "stereophonic richness of the exchange between the sexes" still flourishes in its own way two centuries after de Staël put her own brand of feminist iconoclasm on the map. Personally, I'd never given much thought to "stereophonic richness" while growing up in the States except when fiddling with the woofer

----

*Thus different scents infuse the *air du temps*. In France you have *fraternité*, *paternité*, and *maternité*, but there is no word in the French lexicon for sisterhood, and no shared Ya-Ya cultural reference for it.

In her book *De l'Alcôve à l'Arène*, author Michèle Sarde explains that if French women do indeed love men "a lot, a lot," there's good news and bad news at play. The good news is that French women have generally been happy to "embellish their homes and their beds for them" over the decades and the centuries. The bad news is that they "have so loved their men, fathers, sons, brothers, and lovers or husbands to such an extent, that they've neglected to love one another." French women "continue to maintain toward their own gender a reductive and condescending regard from which they themselves, each one of them, have individually suffered."

In other words those femmes fatales can be fatal to one another, which explains the chill of permafrost that sometimes lingers around them.

----

on a car radio, though even in the playgrounds of my youth and during some of feminism's brightest moments, I could recall the enduring seeds of "homosociality" in the way boys and girls were often segregated. (The day we were ushered into the school auditorium with the solemnity of a slightly alarming liturgical rite to watch gender-specific sex education films comes immediately to mind.)

Like Alain Giami, Madame de Staël had a point, and it's interesting to note how that point has been observed by those who followed in her footsteps. A quick sampling of quotes over the centuries:

Alexis de Tocqueville took one good hard look at America's growing colonies and noted: "America is the one country in the world where the most continual care has been taken to trace clearly separated lines of action for the two sexes, and where the wish is for them to walk with equal steps, but always on different paths."

Living in France, Edith Wharton observed her American sisters from afar and offered these harsh words: "It is because American women are each other's only audience, and to a great extent each other's only companions, that they seem, compared to women who play an intellectual and social part in the lives of men, like children in a baby school." (Ouch.)

When things got existential in France, Simone de

Beauvoir visited the United States and recoiled at the manner in which American men and women seemed to occupy two different social spheres. Writes Ozouf of de Beauvoir: "Invited to dinner in the United States by two independent young women not sporting wedding rings, she sighed: the apartment smelled of the single life, the dinner was bathed in 'a bitter absence,' that meal among women was a sad meal without men. She saw the ordinary separation of the sexes in America as the reason for American women's attitude of defiance toward men, whom they considered enemies. . . . She remained faithful to her experience of an easy, relaxed relation with men—happy."

Easy. Relaxed. Happy. Hello?

Two

MYSTERY

On shades of gray, what it means to live with an infinite gamut of romance, the power of the Implicit, the perils of the "date," the seductive virtues of the inner life, what it means when less really is more, and why it's not how you tie a scarf that counts but what's in your head when you wear it

*Not necessarily for their age or beauty, but
what really motivates the civilized man
is the curiosity aroused by mystery and
obstacle.*

—PROUST

*Love is a phenomenon susceptible of innu-
merable variations.*

—RAOUL DE ROUSSY DE SALES

Truth is in nuances.

—BENJAMIN CONSTANT

Love is blind and hindsight is 20/20. No wonder we've got problems. The French have their own idioms about love, of course, but there's one above all others that illuminates how differently they look at love and what it means to live with "an infinite gamut of romance." I stumbled on it by accident when I met Sandrine in the Buttes Chaumont Park in Paris one fall day. Sandrine was a thirteen-year-old French girl who, among other preoccupations, was enamored of a boy named Pierre. After a short conversation about Pierre's abundant qualities (he could, it turns out, recite poems in Gaelic), Sandrine picked a flower and started pulling off its petals. To my surprise, however, rather than the familiar refrain, "He loves me, he loves me not. He loves me, he loves me not," Sandrine carefully intoned: "He loves me a little, a lot, passionately, madly, not at all" (*Il m'aime un peu, beaucoup, passionnement, à la folie, pas du tout*). I instantly thought that Sandrine was one clever little girl until I learned that, no, this is the standard French refrain. This is how French girls have been thinking about love forever:

He loves me a little.

A lot.

Passionately.

Madly.

Not at all.

How unfair. While we Anglo girls are stuck in the absolutes of total love or utter rejection, the French girl is already primed to think in nuances and in an infinite gamut of romance. While we lust after happy endings and closure, they're comfortable with emotional subtleties and ambiguity. While we grow up thinking in black and white, they grow up inscrutably gray.

As I recalled the petal-picking days of my own American youth, I couldn't help but wonder what my life might have been like, had it been lived out in those bewitching shades of gray. Let's take this potent little flower metaphor and trek through a few of those shades.

In Stephen Clarke's novel *A Year in the Merde*, Paul West is a British executive on assignment in France. With lust in his loins and sex on his mind, our friend desperately tries to "shag" a French woman—in vain. Confused yet seduced by the nuanced ways of French women, he laments: "I really couldn't figure out French women. Were they fans of mental foreplay? Only into intellectual sex? Or did they want to be

----

jumped on?" Apparently, nobody told our horny Brit about shades of gray, so we'll just do it for him:

French women generally hold their cards close at hand. They don't wear their hearts on their shirtsleeves, and they won't tell you or Oprah their life story in five minutes. They won't reveal who's been visiting their secret garden or even tell you where they bought their skirt on sale, and, while we're at it, they won't wait patiently in line (yes, it *is* genetic). That's because French women—and men, for that matter—are private, not public. They have an enormous sense of personal boundaries and their secret gardens bloom not in the harsh glare of sunlight but in the coolness of those shades of gray. *If French women are so hot,* our Brit might as well have asked, *why do they seem so cold?* This may explain why. They favor the implicit over the explicit; the subtext over the context; discretion over indiscretion; and the hidden is often much more enticing than the obvious. In other words, they're exactly the opposite of Anglos.

Now I regret that, given our national addiction to the black and white, there is no clear-cut, direct path through all of this. It would be much easier to tackle something concrete, like, say, scarves. The way French women wear their scarves has fascinated non-French women worldwide. What is it about the scarf? It is the emblem of sophisticated nonchalance that only French women seem to master. The sexy woman in a convertible, driving along the Mediterranean coast with her lover, always invariably wears a scarf—a frighteningly long silk one that flutters behind her like a wedding veil gone wild. In fact, the scarf is just the opposite of the wedding veil. The wedding veil says: I am here as a precious dynastic symbol of the immutable ties that will bind me to my spouse for all eternity till death do us part. The scarf says: To hell with all that.

The scarf's seductive appeal is so great that it enjoys an entire body of literature dedicated to scarf-tying, not to mention its own entry in Wikipedia, but guess what? It's not the ability to tie a scarf *comme ça* that gives French women their seductive cachet, nor is it the ability to look sexy with no makeup or simultaneously consume pastry, foie gras, and cheese and Not Get Fat. No. It is something far simpler yet far more complex.

It is this: Less Is More.

Of course, we've all heard this pithy phrase, and what, pray tell, does it really mean? In our trek through these gray zones we need to *reverse* the phrase and think of it this way: When Less is More, you often get More with Less. More passion with less planning. More love and intimacy with less information and grief. More freedom with less fretting. And, yes, while we're at it, more style with less stuff.

To illustrate this wanton principle, consider the film by French director Claire Denis called *Friday Night*. A man is stuck in his car in one of those massive Parisian traffic jams that make you want to retire to a mobile home community in the desert. A young woman walks down the street, gets in the man's car, and basically hitches a ride. (Never mind that in that kind of traffic she could walk to Madrid faster than it

----

would take them to cross the Seine.) They sit in silence for nearly the duration of the film. Eventually, they end up in a hotel. They make love rhapsodically, speak in French haiku over pizza, make love again, then say good-bye. What just happened? After her encounter, our leading lady (deliciously *jolie laide* by the way) runs through the streets of Paris alone toward an unknown future. Her face is lit with a strangely happy glow. She's just left her mysterious lover in the hotel and she doesn't even know his name. What kind of date was that? Who is he? What does he do for a living? Will she see him again? Was this a one-night stand or the beginning of a long-term relationship? Did she even get his cell-phone number, for crying out loud?

Our French heroine doesn't seem to give a damn, but *we* sure do. We sure do because we do not like ambiguity. We do not like not knowing. We do not appreciate seemingly Random Acts of Love and Sex unless they come from George Clooney. We're not particularly fond of any infinite gamuts of romance unless we know exactly where those annoying gamuts are going, because rather than setting things in motion, we Anglos prefer to set things in stone, with clear objectives, goals, and outcomes. Is he my soul mate or my future husband? Does He Love Me or Does He Love Me Not?

A veritable onslaught of love advice is at our disposal to answer those questions, all well-intentioned and perfectly suited to extinguish all opportunities for unexpected personal alchemy and gag the life out of experiences that might not lead to marriage but would still ripen one's sensibilities. Such experiences, inherently gray by nature, tend to die on the vine with such precision. And what's left in our lonely gardens are consensual or prenup relationship agreements and one unsexy legal definition for the word *date* that's been set in stone by a San Francisco appellate court as the following: "a social relationship between two individuals who have a reciprocally amorous and increasingly exclusive interest in one another, and shared expectation of the growth of that mutual interest, that has endured for such a length of time and stimulated such frequent interactions that the relationship cannot be deemed to have been casual."

Excusez-moi?

Now, I adore having "reciprocally amorous and increasingly exclusive interests." Who doesn't? When I was younger, they were my raison d'être and "going steady" was my ultimate goal. There was something about the ring of "going steady" that had the permanence of granite written all over it. My boyfriend and I are *going steady*. We are a train moving *steadily* toward a predetermined station, that station being marriage. Never mind that I was fourteen, my boyfriend still had braces, and our peers were desperately preoccupied with acne or tampons (when they weren't desperately preoccupied with going steady). Going steady suggested an invincible steadiness in the face of any emotional fly ball that might come hurtling out of left field, and everyone played the game of love, trying to avoid those balls and get to home base as quickly as possible. How little that changes as "relationship experts" and love gurus guide us as adults through the hinterland of the heart with rules, strategies, and techniques to win the game of love.

Such is not the case in France, which is not to say that French women aren't addicted to love. Their hearts thump madly with desire like everyone else's; that said, they don't need relationships so tightly defined from the get-go, self-help love advice is not as big on their emotional agendas, they have an uncanny tolerance for ambiguity and mystery, and they basically don't appreciate the Anglo penchant for setting things in stone.

My first whiff of this came when I met a young French man here in America. He was an exchange student from one of those elite schools in Paris, the kind you're born into before you are actually born, presumably through ancestral connections that date back to King Charlemagne. I immediately knew that he was French because he managed to wear socks with sandals and not look ridiculous. His name was Jean-Marc, and I deeply adored him for the hyphen alone. Jean. Hyphen. Marc. There was something so appealing to me at the time about French people who got to enjoy compound names, as if they were two-in-one and fully loaded. Marie. Hyphen. Claire. Jean. Hyphen. Marc.

Anyhow, one day Jean-Marc sat next to me in a university auditorium where we were both students. After listening to the cryptic incantations of a semiotics professor, he invited

----

me to lunch. I accepted. He took me to a little café and was exceptionally gallant. He opened the door for me. He picked up the tab. He demurred in every way. I found this so wildly old-fashioned that it was almost a turnoff. We spent the afternoon together and ended up in my apartment. And then Jean-Marc did another gallant thing: he made me dinner in my own kitchen. Now this was back when America had only one Galloping Gourmet and masculinity was defined by what you *didn't* know about cuisine, and in this context Jean-Marc seemed positively queer in every sense of the word. Which brings me to a very brief digression about French men.

Let's admit it: French men *do* have a way of veering away from typical Anglo male stereotypes. Henry James once remarked that the average French man is "of so different a type from the average Englishman that you can easily believe that to the end of time the two will not understand each other." That goes a long way in explaining why you can always spot French guys, particularly on an American beach: they're the ones wearing peanut-sized bathing suits instead of knee-long baggy trunks ample enough to house a family of chipmunks. French guys also kiss on the cheeks, they wear scarves, they know how to cook, they've all read Proust and—get this—according to a poll in the French edition of *Enfant* magazine, 38 percent of them wish they could get pregnant (100 percent of French women undoubtedly wish the same thing).

However, do not be fooled. Despite what Anglos might

consider feminine attributes (hey, dude, what's with the bikini bottoms?), French men are still as macho and interested in their male anatomy as any other Tom, Dick, or Harry. But as my friend Nathalie put it: "French guys don't feel the need to prove their virility in the same way. To be manly, French guys don't have to drink beer, play football, or otherwise play up to the same sorts of traditional male stereotypes that exist in the States."

Jean-Benoît Nadeau of *Sixty Million Frenchmen Can't Be Wrong* fame provides a historical side dish, suggesting that some of these manly metaphors go back to the nineteenth century when, as he said to me over the phone, "Americans used to go to France to entrench themselves in the values of the Renaissance man: poetry, speaking French, learning about art and how to fence. But after the 1850s there was a reversal. The Renaissance man slowly became the Marlboro Man. Guys went to France, not to get schooled in the arts, but to get laid, to get debauched. Men who were at all ambiguous or too Renaissance were suspect. When I was growing up, we used to say about an ambiguous guy, 'He's either European or he's gay.' But I've noticed that in France, police and firemen and SWAT guys are not necessarily beefy like in the States. In France, beefy is gay. . . . in France these Renaissance attributes prevail, and [this] must have an impact on how people experience love and sex."

Sure it does. In a culture where fewer staunchly defined notions of masculine/feminine segregate the sexes, people have got more room to be who they are within the context of their own gender, and everyone is bound to experience love and sex with more joy and freedom.

But back to Jean-Marc. In one of the more enduring moments of my young adulthood, my new French friend decided to make a cassoulet for me that first night in my own kitchen. Now I feel obliged to confess that back then I didn't actually know what a cassoulet was, nor where you might find half of the ingredients to make one. (Writing this feels slightly scandalous, like admitting that you haven't read Harry Potter or that you forgot to wear underwear to your graduation ceremony.) Back then, my refrigerator was an homage to California's health-food fanaticism, stocked with everything from wheat juice and suspicious-looking cleansers to vitamins the size of lemons and bins of alfalfa sprouts. (Jean-Marc took one look at those fuzzy little sprouts and said, "This is what French people feed their livestock.") Personally, I wasn't exactly sure what a flageolet was—bean? sixteenth-century woodwind instrument?—though to my credit I *did* have a large, sturdy earthenware pot. I used it, however, as a fruit bowl. Jean-Marc looked around and shook his head. This was one unsexy kitchen.

Eventually, Jean-Marc did manage to find everything he needed except goose fat (I drew the line at goose fat back then. I erased it shortly thereafter), and in the span of an evening I went from Lapsed Vegetarian to Curious Carnivore. I'm not sure if I even knew Jean-Marc's last name at the time, and if

I did, I probably wouldn't have been able to pronounce it. I won't tell you if I slept with him that first night because that would be immoral and I'm saving myself for chapter 3. The point is that I didn't know much about Jean-Marc when he eventually suggested that I return with him to Paris. I did not have enough information about him. We had not gone through the proper dating protocol. The future could not be pinned down without it. If I went to Paris with him, would he be my soul mate, my husband, or simply the subject of future cocktail conversation? Was this a path to going steady or going unsteady?

Long hours ensued during which time my girlfriends deconstructed every excruciating detail about my relationship with Frenchie according to the latest self-help love gospel on the market. My mind seems to have blocked all neurotransmitters that might refire any memory of who exactly was writing that love advice, but clearly running off to a foreign country with a French stranger (one who did indeed wear bikini bottoms and read Proust) was not high on the list of twelve steps, six rules, seven tools, or nine handy keys to success in love. Thus, the only overriding questions that prevailed as we retraced every moment I'd spent with Jean-Marc were: What does everything *mean*? and Where is this relationship *going*? The answers to which were: *nothing at the moment*, and *who knows*?

In the end my friends were divided. Half of them responded with, "Oh. My. God. He lives in *Paaah*-ris! What are you waiting for?" The other half shouted, "Are you nuts?"

- - - - - - - - -

French philosopher Pascal once said that "the heart has its reasons which reason ignores." That's a much nicer way of saying that ignorance is bliss. Six months later I was on an Air France flight to Paris. I traveled lightly—one leather jacket, a few woolly sweaters, some jeans, a battered but beloved Larousse dictionary, and—don't ask me why—a pair of rubber thongs (the kind you wear on your feet; I just had to make that clear)—but I carried my weight in cultural baggage.

Even with all prior hand-wringing speculation, I walked into Jean-Marc's French life not realizing that he had, well, a life, and that that life included French women. Many of them. Clusters of them, in fact, who clung to him like grapes, offering lots of that sexy ambiguous complicity and probably a few savory cassoulets of their own. They certainly looked like they had a lot of experience with those infinite gamuts of romance. These women were not coquettes as French women are often stereotyped, but they did seem to have an inexhaustible supply of feminine guile, and next to their sophisticated ways I felt ten years younger, which is not a good thing when you're barely twenty. They also did seem to love men *a lot, a lot.* Particularly one woman named Chloe. Who seemed to particularly love Jean-Marc. *A lot. A lot.*

Chloe had short-cropped hair and a fabulously forthright Roman nose; she was no great beauty but she did have great legs, which she took equally great pains to highlight, usually in a very black miniskirt. Like her French sisters, she grew up marinating in all that voluptuous male/female complicity we described in our previous chapter, which made my fat-free, gender-neutral past seem a little, well, bland. It also made her relationship with Jean-Marc confusing. They laughed over little nothings; Chloe would put her hands on Jean-Marc's hips and gently nudge him aside as she made her way through the constricted hallway in his apartment—a gesture that had unbearable sexual heft to me. Were they just friends or "friends with benefits"? Had they ever "gone steady"? The very term uttered in this French context, where an ambient sensuality hung over everything like a thundercloud packed with imminent rain, seemed painfully childish.

That said, one evening, after too many glasses of Côtes du Rhône, I tried to bumble my way into Chloe's heart for clarity, unaware that my desire for knowing and revealing might be rivaled by her penchant for abstraction and restraint. Our conversation went something like this:

ME: So, Chloe, how long have you known Jean-Marc?

CHLOE: Jean-Marc? Oh, we have known each other a long time.

ME: So, you guys were at one point, you know, boyfriend and girlfriend?

CHLOE: What does this mean, "boyfriend and girlfriend"?

ME: It means, well, you know, you were *committed* to each other.

CHLOE: What does this mean, "committed"?

ME (*Oh, Lord*): Well, "committed" means that you only see
the other person. It means that you're in an exclusive
relationship that doesn't include other people.

CHLOE: What is the point of that?

ME: The point is that . . . that . . . (*what the—?*) . . . that you
only want to see that other person because you're, like I
said, boyfriend and girlfriend.

CHLOE: So, we are back to the first point?

ME: I guess we are.

CHLOE: And what is the point of *that*?

ME (*Where is Robespierre when you need him?*): What is
the point of anything?

CHLOE: Precisely. Very good question.

At this point Chloe lit a cigarette, ran her hands through her
hair, and looked at me with a trace of . . . annoyance? Amusement? Or was it affection? Was she joking or was she seriously
clueless? Was this the beginning of a fabulous friendship
or was it simply extreme disdain masking itself as indifference? Her face told me nothing. Here we had a case of More
Mystery with Fewer Facial Expressions. I felt a little like Kate
(Meg Ryan) in the film *French Kiss*: Kate goes to Paris in the
footsteps of her American fiancé, who's run off with an elusive and sexy French woman. Stumped by the inscrutable
Frog Queen, she can't understand why French women aren't
clearer and more demonstrative with their emotions. To her
new French friend Luc (Kevin Klein with his best French

accent), she remarks: "Happy, smile. Sad, frown. Use the corresponding face with the corresponding emotion. But no. You want this mysterious. . . ." This mysterious *je ne sais quoi*, Ryan would have said, had she not been interrupted.

ME (*Stupidly pressing on*): Well, did you guys ever date?

CHLOE (*Blank stare*): "Date"? What is this thing called "date"?

ME: You're kidding, right?

CHLOE (*Long drag from cigarette, dramatic exhale*): Is this a thing that Americans do?

ME: What "thing"?

CHLOE: This thing where you must know everything. This thing where you must have everything tied together and put into a little box so that you can understand it and control it.

ME: I'm not interested in any little box or in controlling anything.

CHLOE: Good. Neither am I. So we agree.

At which point she smiled, at last, and walked away. The thought of Chloe still gives me high blood pressure.

Which brings us to another cultural riff the size of Mont Blanc. Nothing illustrates more clearly the French woman's tolerance for accepting ambiguity, even as she plunges headfirst into Cupid's wicked arms, more than the way she approaches the world of dating. Ask any French woman how she dates and she'll look at you with a blank stare. Or she might sniff, as my friend Véronique once did, and say, "I don't 'do dates.' That is an Anglo-Saxon concept." So what exactly do French women do?

Let us first begin with a disclaimer: there are nearly one million French singles who, like their Anglo counterparts, troll the Internet for love interests, blinking and blazing through cyber superstores in the hopes of finding a possible boyfriend, lover, or husband. There is blogging and bar-hopping and millions who watch prime-time French TV shows like *C'est quoi l'amour?* (What's Love?) and *L'île de tentation* (Temptation Island), where French babes and their hunky man-frogs try to seduce one another's mates on a Kon-Tiki island that would make the *Love Boat* captain weep. Inspired by the worst American fare, the show has love connection cafés and speed dating and "relookers" and even an Ecole de Séduction, which in the land of seduction seems about as cheesy as an overripe hunk of Brie. France brims with enough singles to populate the entire state of Arizona, so what do French women know about dating and the travails of Cupid's arrow that we don't?

> *Boy, those French. They have a different word for everything.*
>
> —STEVE MARTIN

First off, there is literally no word or concept for "date" in France. Look it up in a Franco-American dictionary and you will simply get the word *sortir*, which means "to go out." Ah, what a relief. In France you just "go out with" someone. You might go to a café and talk about French bulldogs or you might end up in a seventeenth-century farmhouse and make passionate love on a bale of hay while your lover recites Mallarmé. There is no explicit how-to formula here. There are no dating tools, twelve steps, or action plans in the French woman's world. There is no right or wrong way to "date." Until quite recently there were few books, except those translated from English, exhorting them to "package" or "brand" themselves like heirloom tomatoes, with love advice pulled from marketing dogma that is as sexy and life-affirming as a Profit & Loss statement.

Thus the French—women and men—are baffled when they land on American soil and start to "date." One French man tried his best to explain the concept in a New York blog for French expatriates. "After ten years of this %$*@!?! word called 'date,'" he wrote, "I have arrived at the following conclusion." And here it is:

"A date is a verb and a noun

It is not necessarily a prelude to a relationship

To date: 'The act of being in (or wanting) a relationship'

To go on a date: 'an appointment'

Now, you may not say to your partner: 'I would like to date you' or 'Let's go on a date.' Generally, the response is: 'I am not looking for a relationship.' But after making

----

an appointment with someone, you may say, 'It's a date, then.'"

Other French veterans of the American dating scene responded to this with personal advice: *"A 'date' is like a job interview. Things turn around money. Everything is ultracodified,"* one blogger wrote. To which another replied with: *"No matter how much you both want each other, don't ever suggest to a guy that you'll go to his house on a first 'date' or you'll be accused of being a 'bad girl' or wanting a 'one-night stand.'"* Yet another dater warned: *"Don't ever call someone three times the day after a date even if you're both crazy about one another. . . ."* And then came a final piece of advice: *"1. You must have an opinion. 2. That opinion must be the same as your American date's."*

Deconstructing the phenomenon in greater detail for the French in an essay called "Date-ology: A User's Guide," blogger Cyril explains that an American date "is a permanent maneuver to have the maximum of choice." It involves "pursuing several 'dates' at the same time to analyze the compatibility quotient between different candidates" and will often require the assistance of "the lawyer of both parties, a financial adviser, a psychoanalyst, a nutritionist, a yoga instructor, an insurance agent, ten industrial-strength disinfectants, and blood test results." So impenetrable is the concept of the American date that even French philosopher Bernard-Henri Lévy, or BHL as the French call him with equal doses of affection and derision, had his two centimes to add: "This [American] system of dating, relationships, evaluating, and getting married is too formal and excessively ritualized, resulting in a loss of mystery," he once told an interviewer. "It is an example of American Puritanism, this manner of separating things, of the excessive codification of love."

Further complicating matters for the French is the American bias to lay all your cards on the table when you date. You will never see, for example, a French cartoon like the one that recently appeared in *The New Yorker*, where a couple is sitting in a restaurant and the man is saying, "No, I don't think we need counseling. This is our first date." That's because the cartoon implies that great heaps of personal dysfunction have already been shared on a first date. This rarely happens in the French woman's world. While the French love their shrinks, the self-help gestalt that advocates public confessionals is not a fixture in their daily lives and even couples therapy has yet to become a household word. The politics of seduction are woven into the realm of the implicit, and the dance between two people is not a connect-the-dots exercise in tell-all intimacy, but rather, as Françoise Giroud once said, "the act of offering oneself and holding back; giving and remaining aloof, for an odd mix of playfulness and reticence."

With this in mind it was in a haze of channel-surfing boredom that I stumbled on the TV show *The Bachelor: Paris*. Here, twenty-five single American women pony up to one American bachelor for the ultimate date in Paris (that would be a date that quickly leads to wedding bells—equally bizarre to the French, but we'll get to that). Not much room for any "odd mix of anything," let alone any "infinite gamut of romance." Everything codified and dreadful about our dating culture is gelled into this half-hour slot of Hallmark romance, including the strangely Victorian final leg of the show, when the two runners-up (after a tear-filled whittling away of the congenially hopeful contestants) are questioned by the Bachelor's entourage—blue-blood mom, dour dad, suspicious sister, clueless brother-in-law—to see how neatly they might fit in the box with Mr. Bachelor. In this stressful scenario, love is an Extreme Sport in a world of high-stakes dating, and you can almost feel dread coursing through your *own* veins (you're suddenly sixteen years old again and possibly going steady) as the contestants, each one beauty pageant-perfect, song-and-dances her way into the Bachelor's heart, desperately hoping to pick the right petal (*he loves me!*) in this Winner Takes All game.

Of these antics our French women might wonder not only why this grown man couldn't make up his own mind, how many simultaneous "dates" were required to find "that special someone," or why the world of dating was so utterly stressful; more important, they might wonder if in this world of dreary prefab romance, the Bachelor and his fellow Americans hadn't sold out on love lock, stock, and barrel. They might even ask themselves: Where is fate in all this?

Fate. Now that's a loaded word. Like "yoga" or "karma," it's one of those words that slipped out of its native culture and ended up a celebrity with an extreme makeover. If there's anything that fate implies in this context, it's the ability to let go and embrace the virtues of *not* knowing—of *not* planning and *not* trying to fit too neatly into the box. It is not about He loves me/He loves me not. It is not binary or about how-to. It is not about black/white, right/wrong, love/hate, success/failure. You also can't plan for fate since it's experience-driven, not goal-oriented, and it will always have different plans for you from the ones you make for yourself (and if you don't believe that, you're either too busy planning to notice or you simply haven't lived long enough).

French women have a tendency to live out this principle (or should we call it an "anti-principle"?), which often makes for less fretting and lonely prognosticating about romance, no matter who they are or how old they are. In fact, if there's one thing that's attractive about older French women while we're at it—and the only other stereotype more emblazoned in our minds beside the sexy French woman is the sexy *older* French woman—it's the sense that through life experience they've accrued enough information not to need much of it at all.

If older French women still seem like players in that infinite game of romance, it's mainly because they are comfortable being grown-ups. They act their age. They essentially look their age. They still enjoy seductive pleasures with men their age. Or not. Romantic liaisons with younger men in France generally aren't characterized by the same moral ambivalence or age-defying, age-denying anxiety that goes on in the States. Let's note that the love affair between forty- or fifty-year-olds is a staple in French cinema, as opposed to the junior varsity squad that dominates film in America. The most memorable "older" women in love or lust on the silver screen in America are often either insane (think Glenn Close in *Fatal Attraction*) or alcoholic (think Anne Bancroft in *The Graduate*). Remarkably, it was nearly half a century ago that Mrs. Robinson brought her boozy high-brow grown-up angst to the silver screen, but we can salute this complex, inso- lent older woman (even though, of course, she was a wreck), if only for her defiance of certain middle-class values in her pursuit of passion.

Had Mrs. Robinson been French, she might have had a more serene go of it all. I'm reminded of Nathalie Baye, a French actress and "sexy older French woman" who is roughly Mrs. Robinson's age in the French film *An Affair of Love*. The short version of *An Affair of Love* goes like this: Baye puts an ad in the paper seeking a man exclusively for sex. She's no tart, however. No hint of lewdness taints her quest. She wants pas- sion, a taste of carnal knowledge that will anchor her more deeply to a sense of her own humanity. Within no time, voilà, Sergi López shows up. Now, there are a million things that Baye could worry about when she first meets Lopez: Serial killer? Virus carrier? Garden-variety madman? But the one thing she seems concerned about is whether he's hairy or not. (Rest assured. He is.) The only catch going into the affair for our lovers is this: they must never know each other's name,

----

where they live, what they do for a living, their phone numbers, nothing. Love and sex get tangled up in messy sheets, blue hotel rooms, and serious bathtubs, and hearts are entwined in a mesh of longing and curiosity, yet mystery hangs over everything, suspended in midair like a lenticular cloud.

When Baye and López finally declare their love for each other (because love eventually does seep in through the cracks), we desperately want them to get on with a "real" relationship—you know, the kind with "real" dates and barbecues and vacation plans and wedding bells tinkling in the distance. But eventually they come to the same desperately reasonable conclusion: that once they truly get to know each other—as the tide of personal information, complexities, and just plain *stuff* surges in and fills up that pristine emotional space they've shared—their love affair will be over. And so they do what any other practically minded, existentially bred French couple might do: they end their relationship right then and there.

To Anglos this generally signals the failure of the whole experience; to these French lovers, however, it only seems to heighten the value of it. For French women it's okay if the emotional integrity of a relationship lies in the experience of it alone and not necessarily in its outcome or ultimate resolution (he loves me/he loves me not). There is a willingness here, *très français*, to contemplate or accept an experience that doesn't necessarily go anywhere in particular—no closure, folks—but that is still an essential and necessary part of love, sex, and being human.

This, of course, is categorically Not Okay in our culture. Your girlfriend would not get it. Your mother would not approve. "Relationship experts" would veto the whole thing. No matter how sexy an encounter might be, nobody wants to find herself like Maria Schneider in *Last Tango in Paris*.

> MARIA SCHNEIDER: I don't know what to call you.
>
> MARLON BRANDO: I don't have a name.
>
> SCHNEIDER: Do you want to know my name?
>
> BRANDO: No. I don't want to know your name. You don't have
> a name and I don't have a name, either. No names here.
> Not one name.

Talk about more sex with less information.

If deep-seated desires and entrenched realities are reflected in our mass entertainment, contrasting Nathalie Baye in *An Affair of Love* with Diane Keaton in *Something's Gotta Give* is an exercise in pop anthropology. Both films were produced at roughly the same time and feature actresses who play women in their late prime. And yet where Nathalie Baye is open to life and passion, Keaton plays a self-described "high-strung, overamped, controlling, know-it-all neurotic" named Erica, who wears turtlenecks in the summer and who, when love and sex unexpectedly enter her life, gets so busy micromanaging her world and her countless insecurities that she's like a four-wheel drive vehicle with torque, traction, and wheel slip functions in high gear. Erica is courted by not one man but *two*: a cheeky older man her age named Harry (the swinging Jack Nicholson) and a younger, hottie doctor many years her junior named Julian (the primly handsome Keanu Reeves). With two men on the ranch, one hopes Erica will hitch her pony to at least one of them. But no. Life could bonk her over the head with an infinite gamut of romance and she wouldn't notice.

"You really are a very sexy woman," Mr. Sexy Doctor himself tells her. To which she protests, "No, really, swear to God, I'm NOT."

And when a little hanky-panky actually *does* take place with Harry, well, things are a little confusing:

ERICA: You know what, Harry? If it's all right with you, I'd rather like to be friends.

HARRY: Friends? I'm not ready to be your FRIEND!

ERICA: Fine, I understand.

HARRY: And, anyway, do you really buy that horseshit that a man and a woman can be friends after they've had sex?

ERICA: I'm friends with my ex-husband, but, then again, we didn't just have sex.

HARRY: We didn't just have sex, either.

ERICA: Then what was it? I'd love to know.

HARRY: Can I e-mail it to ya when I figure it out?

- - - - - - - - - -

I'm reminded of a recent *New Yorker* cartoon: A man and woman are naked in bed. The woman says: "I'm confused. Is this the start of something, the end of something, or the whole something?" All this bafflement over sex is funny and makes sense to us. To the French it's simply bewildering.

When love and sex walk in the room in America, something's gotta give or something's at least gotta be clear. We don't want ambiguity or mystery, and we certainly don't want to keep that tide of personal information at bay. Au contraire, we like to open the floodgates. Show and Tell. Get the Big Reveal. You know what I'm talking about. I was recently at a cocktail party in the States when the hostess asked all of us guests to get in a circle with our margaritas and tell the group about the most meaningful and powerful personal experience we'd ever had. One woman with a full head of meaningful and powerful red hair shot up and said, "The first time I had a multiple orgasm!"

Really—must we know this? Must we put our orgasms on the slab for public inspection? Ask a French woman the same question and she'll look at you like you asked her to strip naked on a national highway and sing "La Marseillaise." In Swahili. Similarly, while everyone in America seems to have something to shout about—whether they're having *Mind-Blowing Sex*! or whether their libido has gone into early retirement in a time-share condo in Florida—the national appetite for the how-to is an acquired taste the French find, well, distasteful. In his book *French and Americans: The*

Other Shore, French consultant Pascal Baudry cites a major American sex report that "identified some fifty steps in the progress toward intercourse." Baudry suggests that the cultural differences between the French and Americans in this matter "are so great that the mere mention of this finding is enough to make French readers feel that Americans are truly ridiculous."

What's ridiculous, if I may boldly extrapolate, is the childlike need for the Loudly Instructional, which is not to say that the French don't have their share of sex gurus and how-to advice. They do. They have Brigitte Lahaie, among others, a former porn star turned sex therapist who doles out remarkably sober and contemplative sex advice to goat farmers and executives alike on national radio. There is also Dr. Gérard Leleu, who, if you can imagine it, is what Dr. Phil might be like if he were a French sex therapist.

It's also not to ignore the legacy of graphic literary erotica that the French have bequeathed us, starting with the nasty old Marquis de Sade himself. However, ordinary French people don't come home after a long day at the office and spend the remainder of their evening having torrid orgiastic S&M dinner parties in remote medieval châteaus, nor do they engage in polymorphously perverse "open air fucking" with the kind of multiple strangers who greet us in Catherine Millet's autobiographical tale of existential lust.

When it comes to love and sex, most ordinary French women advocate the idea that when things are too explicit, they tend to cancel out whatever intrinsic value they might have had in the first place. That might be what French philosopher Roland Barthes meant when he said that in America sex is everywhere except in sex. There's a general consensus here that intimacy does not necessarily come when we share all in the interest of achieving total mutual understanding—something right off the bat French women generally consider quixotic, if not something of a killjoy; they are far more inclined to believe that an overly zealous effort to break down boundaries in an effort to create mutual intimacy is what compromises intimacy in the end. "There are some things that do not need to be said," my friend Anne once told me. "They are either too powerful or too painful, and the knowledge of these things often doesn't help the other person. The value of going to a therapist when you're married is not to say everything, to learn how to become One with the other person, but to learn how to stay together as two separate individuals."

In other words, mandated emotional clock-punching and tell-all news bulletins can make the heart grow weary and strained. The libido generally goes along for the ride and heads south. In an essay for *The Atlantic* that takes this to its logical extreme, French journalist Raoul de Roussy de Sales observed, back in the 1930s, what he characterized as an American tendency to strive for moral perfection through "devastating candor." "Truth is an explosive," he wrote, "and it should be handled with care, especially in marital life. It is not necessary to lie, but there is little profit in juggling with hand grenades just to show how brave one is. Secondly, the theory of absolute sincerity presupposes that if love cannot withstand continuous blasting, then it is not worth saving anyway. Some people want their love life to be a permanent Battle of Verdun. When the system of defense is destroyed beyond repair, then the clause of hopeless maladjustment is invoked by one side, or by both. The next thing to do is to divorce and find someone else to be recklessly frank with for a season." De Sales further warns that those committed to the pursuit of absolute and relentless truth-telling risk developing "fiendish traits of character that might otherwise remain dormant."

The ability to hold back the floodgates of personal confession in the interest of remaining a "separate individual," particularly within the context of a couple, is one of those simultaneously fine and infuriating aspects of the French character, for it defies the Anglo desire (can we go so far as to call it a mandate?) to lay all of one's cards on the table in a relationship, or to seduce with a Big Bang rather than a Slow Reveal. It also implies not only a capacity to keep secrets but to cultivate them—and *that* suggests that it's okay for unspoken experiences to coexist that aren't necessarily shared with one's partner. In America, where sharing is considered a moral virtue if not a civic duty, that is also decidedly not okay.

In fact, the French love their secrets. They love the whole

smoky, ambiguous, mysterious cargo of them. Secrets have an invisible alchemy to them; they're personal, potent things with seductive heft and intangible draw. You might not be able to see them or touch them, but you can't see or touch magnetism, either, can you? In his book *Seduction,* Jean Baudrillard, French philosopher and notable "ist" (cultural theorist, postmodernist, poststructuralist, sociologist), described the secret in its extreme abstraction as "The secret: The seductive, initiatory quality of that which cannot be said because it makes no sense, and of that which is not said even though it gets around. Thus, I know another's secret but do not reveal it, and he knows that I know but does not acknowledge it: the intensity between us is simply this secret about the secret."

Got that?

Baudrillard might be impenetrable but he *does* make a point about the seductive cachet of the unspoken. Most Anglos grow up believing that telling secrets is precisely what creates intimacy with someone, not what might compromise it. In fact, when I was younger the only "intensity" I could imagine in a secret unrevealed but commonly acknowledged was the intensity that came from the burning desire to blurt it out. (As de la Rochefoucauld once asked: "How can we expect another to keep our secret if we have been unable to keep it to ourselves?" Remind me to ask myself about that.)

Like many Americans, I grew up in a culture where "sharing" was indeed practically a civic duty. Thus, my own fiend-

---

ish traits of character, nurtured as they were in the Let's Share zeitgeist of California's post-Est hangover, were irrepressible during the early stages of my relationship with my spouse. For example, Mr. Spouse came from a little Burgundian village where proximity to your neighbors was so intense, you had to guard your personal secrets with a vengeance, lest everyone know everything about you. Precisely because I was raised a million cultural light-years away from this village—and because I couldn't get beyond my deep American hankering for full disclosure and the desire to know, well, everything—I was once fiercely interested in knowing the little sexy secrets of my spouse's past love life. Who was his first lover? Was she the daughter of the butcher? The baker? A farm girl or a winsome little tart? Did they do it in a cheese mill? An abandoned fort? How did anyone learn about sex or anything, anyhow, this far from urban civilization? I felt a little like Margaret Mead in Borneo, trying to study the mating habits of an indigenous tribe to get a glimpse of how other people—people who were undoubtedly closer to their instincts and their sexy animal nature than we urbanites—might live and love.

Unfortunately, my husband was unwilling to appease me with answers. To this day I still have no idea about what his youthful sex life might have been like; I only know that he had one, a happy, robust French one, and that is all. The last time I pressed him on the matter, he simply shook his head and said, "Why do you need to know? French women don't need so much information."

- - - - - - - - -

Apparently not.

My own American family displayed equally fiendish traits of character, by the way, the first time my husband had dinner with them. This voluble group asked him a series of questions so probing and personal that, at one point during the course of the evening, he leaned forward and whispered to me, "Is this an inquisition?" The first time I had dinner with his family, on the other hand, it was anything *but* an inquisition. Sitting at a table filled with daunting-looking comestibles I tried to join in the conversation, but despite nearly five hours together, nobody asked me any personal questions at all. Never mind that a cultural rift the size of the Rhone Valley separated us; I was mortified. What faux pas had I committed to merit the silent treatment? Was it the graceless way I'd needled out those tiny and infuriating escargots with their equally tiny and infuriating forks (so much work, so little payback)? Had I used the informal "tu" and thus inadvertently assumed a false intimacy with someone? Or was it something even more deplorable? Whatever it was, it was far from the ebullient cheeriness of my American culture. It was off-putting and even slightly incriminating. It was I'm Okay, You're Not.

"No one asked you personal questions out of *politesse*," my husband explained later. "Out of discretion."

Discretion? Oh. That.

The very word discretion sounds quaint to the American ear in these days of Full Exposure, but it is literally fused into the French brain at birth by virtue of the country's language. Where we have the boldly practical, multipurpose You, they have the complicated linguistic terrain of the formal *vous* and the informal *tu*. For those unfamiliar with French pronouns, *tu* is the familiar form of you—a casual form of conversing that is commonplace in many social contexts. *Vous*, when not used as the plural form of you, is used for anyone you don't know or who merits respect based on age or social status. (Caveat: This does not apply to those rare French individuals who, for reasons that revolve around social class, address their parents in the formal *vous* despite having always had the most informal relations with them.)

Knowing how to navigate *vous* and *tu* with finesse has far more to do with intuition and dancing around subtle social cues than it does with knowing how to conjugate your verbs. I've always been fascinated when a French person suddenly addresses me in the informal *tu* after having addressed me in the formal *vous* for ages. What intangible emotional signals suggesting informality or friendship might have passed between us that I, my brain densely encoded with the generic English *you*, could not fathom? In all my years in France I have never made the leap from the formal *vous* to the informal *tu*; I always took my cues from the other person for fear I might assume a sense of closeness that was not shared. Imagine the horror of suddenly addressing someone with the informal *tu*, only to find that they continue to address you in the formal *vous*. It would feel something like this:

Let's be friends.

No. Let's not.

All this breaks down in the States, of course, where it seems oddly stuffy to use the formal *vous* unless the someone is, say, on a special top-secret diplomatic assignment with the CIA. Americans are practically on a first-name basis with the president of the United States, after all, unlike the French, who when they're not busy vouvoying one another are addressing one another as *madame* or *monsieur*, concealing their first names like ATM codes. In fact, it might be that *tu* is lodged so deeply in our brains—and those imperceptible boundaries so explicitly absent from our vocabulary—that we assume intimate friendship is possible with everyone, and thus will tell total strangers astonishingly personal things that French people wouldn't even tell their shrink.

If the French experience love as an infinite gamut of romance, their language instills in them a sort of built-in radar designed for Instantaneous Intimacy Management. They're able to discern intangible information passed between themselves and others, and negotiate illusive cues that fly right over our Anglophone radars. (I'm reminded of elephants who can hear and communicate with one another through their feet, picking up signals and seismic information that travels through the surface of the ground, makes its way up through their bodies, and filters into their brains. Who knew?)

If there's a gene for this talent—for experiencing more with less, for picking up tiny cues that have larger meaning, and intuiting in a small gesture or detail an entire universe of signification—it must be French. Take Roland Barthes' *A Lover's Discourse*: "A squeeze of the hand—enormous documentation—a tiny gesture within the palm, a knee that does not move away, an arm extended, as if quite naturally, along the back of a sofa and against which the other's head gradually comes to rest—this is the paradisiac realm of subtle and clandestine signs: a kind of festival not of the senses but of meaning." I'm reminded of Eric Rohmer, who dedicated an entire film to the eroticism of Claire's knee.

> *The French have weird ideas about privacy. They think it should be private.*
>
> —BILL MAHER

For French women, silence can be sexy. "Process" is not a verb. If you want to turn a man off, tell him all about yourself or ask him to tell you all about himself. Reveal all. As novelist Camille Laurens puts it somewhat severely: "When you have desire, words are excess baggage. Speaking, in fact, eliminates desire." This is not to put a gag order on love and sex; however, discretion is usually de rigueur in France. It was not, for example, President Sarkozy's sexual antics per se that bothered the French when he divorced his second wife and quickly remarried top model Carla Bruni; it was his willingness, his almost childlike eagerness, to publicly display what is considered private business that they found so distasteful. Trumpeting your private life or otherwise exposing the horticulture blooming in your secret garden is not appreciated by the French.

It's worth noting that privacy is so ingrained in our Gallic friends that even their architecture—its most intriguing spaces concealed behind private courtyards and secret digi-codes—reflects this collective bias. "The French house is a categorical affirmation of its owners' privacy," writes Jean-Benoît Nadeau and Julie Barlow in *Sixty Million Frenchmen Can't Be Wrong*. "You never see the inside of people's homes from the street. Houses in Paris actually turn their backs on the street." So, too, do the French. They turn their backs to the gaze of public life while they covet what goes on behind closed doors, just as they often turn their backs to the outer trappings of surface glam for the seductive virtues of an intriguing inner life. "I love the way she projects two facades," François Truffaut once said of an actress—"a visible one and a subterranean one. She keeps her thoughts to herself; she seems to suggest that her secret, inner life is at least as significant as the appearance she gives."

Well apparently, it *is*. That's the thing about the French: They covet the intellectual and seductive virtues that come with cultivating an inner life. And these virtues imbue their

- - - - - - - - - -

sense of aesthetics. As French actress Isabelle Huppert once told *The Boston Globe*, the French woman's frosty reputation "is a bit of a caricature of the French woman. But of course it's true, compared to the way of behaving that is American. I can understand why it seems iced compared to the way people are here [in America], where so much is exteriorized and so much is obvious and so underlined." Huppert, however, put her finger on something more essential when she suggested that French women also have "the capacity to access something that is elegant yet very simple, without the artifice and seemingly without the effort."

It is fair to assume, all things considered, that this "something"—this implication of knowing radiance that goes beyond the realm of the explicit—is in fact the glimmer of one's inner life.

FRENCH WOMEN KNOW THAT an inner life is a sexy thing. It needs to be nurtured, developed, pampered, soigné. It needs a mani and a pedi on a regular basis. Voltaire once implored the French to cultivate their gardens. He wasn't talking about petunias. There is a distinct advantage, even a dash of snobbery, when you grow up with the cultural mandate that less is truly more (or, inversely, that you can truly get more with less). It is even more brazenly fabulous to look at life, not through a prism of total love or utter rejection, but as a late of possibilities; not as opportunities that fall on a grid, but as experiences that fly on the wings of fate. Who needs a two-note chord (he loves me, he loves me not) when you can have a symphony of nuances and gradations of passion? Who needs the (often disappointing) precision of setting things in stone when you can set things in motion, sometimes with more delightfully messy and potentially intriguing results?

Pascal Baudry once made the observation that when it comes to love and sex, the French "reject things that fit together in a neat and tidy way. You miss all the song and dance that way. You miss the buzz of the bee." Infused with this sensibility, French women not only enjoy that buzz of the bee; many of them are able to embrace the unknown, possibly get shipwrecked on foreign shores, and basically go a little nuts without losing their minds. And this means that they can usually revel in the seas of love without getting battered by the waves and thrown back on the beach with a broken heart and bad hair. They generally refuse to let love and sex be hijacked by rules designed to keep the risks of life at bay, because if there's one thing that French women know, it's this: rules are often meant to be broken.

Three

RULES

On why rules are made to be broken and the wisdom of not believing everything you hear, to balancing romance with realism, and why all this infuses French women with an awareness of the brevity of time and the immediacy of pleasure

Resist, keep resisting, and find the center of your support in yourself.

—MADAME DE STAËL

All I've done my whole life is disobey.

—EDITH PIAF

Welcome to the Georges Hermant pool in Paris. It's one of those summer days so hot and humid you could slice the air with a Laguiole butter knife. Parisians, liberated from the gloom of a long continental winter, have happily cast off their heavy coats and leather gloves for the toasty pleasures of topless sun-worshipping, and the pool teems with humanity. The only official rule here is prominently displayed in the front vestibule: NO SWIMMING TRUNKS. This fashion dictate, which comes not from pool management but all the way from city council itself, is in effect in public pools all over France, presumably to prevent people from swimming in pants and dress shoes and for obscure reasons of hygiene. Only Speedo-type bikinis are permitted for men, which means that your average American guy has to shed a lot more than just his swimming trunks to chill out in this town.

Beyond this one rule it is *liberté*, *égalité*, and *fraternité* at the pool. The locker and shower rooms are coed, and the

----

display of public promiscuity would send any good-hearted Puritan running for the hills. There are also no wall plaques listing the Ten Pool Commandments and no lane dividers for lap swimming, which makes the pool look like the Arc de Triomphe during a rush-hour pileup. When I ask the lone lifeguard on duty about the latter point, he probably doesn't realize that his reply could pretty well sum up the national French ethos. "But, Madame," he says, looking rather shocked, "lane dividers would be an infringement on the individual rights of people to swim as they like."

As I stand at the edge of this pool party and ponder jumping in (the prospect of which looks like jumping into a Hieronymus Bosch painting in your underwear), I realize that France is a sort of inverse daguerreotype of America: in France the rules that are respected are not necessarily the ones posted in public spaces to enforce law and orderly conduct. Rather, they're the unspoken ones that are learned by living in a culture where protocol is upheld by history and tradition. The relative lack of tradition in America, on the other hand, gives Americans the freedom to reinvent themselves in ways that are inconceivable to the French (until recently, for example, the idea of a midlife career change was unthinkable in France). Nevertheless, our rules are clearly spelled out. And we obey them. We stand in lines. We signal when we change lanes. We worship all that self-help advice and play by the book (we *believe* in the book). When we don't, we sue you for everything you're worth; then we get an Extreme Makeover.

Now, don't get me wrong. I think rules are important. I love lane dividers. (What about the individual rights of lap swimmers to swim in a straight line? I wanted to ask that lifeguard.) I'm often annoyed by—and when I'm not, I'm amazed at— the intransigence of the French and their uncanny ability to balance that fine line between being an "individualist" (a French mantra) and being an egotist (the French mantra's id). In any case it is fair to say that the French do not like rules. They do not wait patiently in lines. They do not curb their dogs. They do not observe NO SMOKING signs. They do not drive sanely. (French friends on visit to the States are consistently surprised when American drivers stop at a four-way intersection and are so consumed with cordially waving the others forward that nobody advances across the street.) When Euro Disney published its dress codes for employees, an insurrection practically ensued.

Yes, rules help us all get along, stand in line, and basically Have a Nice Day! without killing one another. They are important. To a point. But when rules start to impinge on our sense of personal freedom, so most French women would be inclined to tell you—or when rules become strident forms of moral dogma and social conventions that are not particularly life-affirming, realistic, or conducive to passion and authenticity—we have a little problem. And if French women appear unapologetically self-possessed when it comes to matters of the heart and the realm of the senses, it is for this reason. They almost categorically challenge rules and institutional dogma that get in the

- - - - - - - - -

way of their sense of pleasure and personal freedom, particularly when it comes to love and sex.

Imagine, for example, that you have sailed the high seas of love and Match.com. You have weathered the tempests of bad dates with zero chemistry. Finally you meet Him. You pick the right petal (He loves me!) and find the Man Who Would Be Husband. You are now thinking seriously of tying the knot, and we're not talking about a scarf. You are about to get married, and a life of committed happiness, security, and rolled-over 401(k) plans is poised to unfold before you.

But wait. You think you know this man—but do you *really*? Does he know *you*, like in that what-if-long-term-you-never-know kind of way? You could be fooling yourself. *He* could be fooling *you*. Here are a few details that you might want to consider before you cross that threshold. In fact, let's not call them details. Let's call them fifteen "key" and "critical questions" that are "ground rules for marriage."

Please take out your No. 2 pencils and answer these questions brought to us by *The New York Times* in a recent article about marriage:

1. Have we discussed whether or not to have children, and if the answer is yes, who is going to be the primary caregiver?

2. Do we have a clear idea of each other's financial obligations and goals, and do our ideas about spending and saving mesh?

- - - - - - - - -

3. Have we discussed our expectations for how the household will be maintained, and are we in agreement on who will manage the chores?

4. Have we fully disclosed our health histories, both physical and mental?

5. Is my partner affectionate to the degree that I expect?

6. Can we comfortably and openly discuss our sexual needs, preferences, and fears?

7. Will there be a television in the bedroom?

8. Do we truly listen to each other and fairly consider one another's ideas and complaints?

9. Have we reached a clear understanding of each other's spiritual beliefs and needs, and have we discussed when and how our children will be exposed to religious/moral education?

10. Do we like and respect each other's friends?

11. Do we value and respect each other's parents, and is either of us concerned about whether the parents will interfere with the relationship?

12. What does my family do that annoys you?

13. Are there some things that you and I are NOT prepared to give up in the marriage?

14. If one of us were to be offered a career opportunity in a location far from the other's family, are we prepared to move?

15. Does each of us feel fully confident in the other's commitment to the marriage and believe that the bond can survive whatever challenges we may face?

This list of "ground rules for marriage" is brought to us by "relationship experts" associated with an "independent marriage-education organization" called PAIRS—or the Practical Application of Intimate Relationship Skills—and they are designed to foresee, control, or prevent all future emotional, physical, domestic, moral, spiritual, behavioral, or financial risks that might pop up on the road of marriage, no matter how big or small. Strangely enough the article is titled "Marriage Is Not Built on Surprises."

French women, smiling wryly into their wineglasses, might suggest that anyone who submits their mate to this challenge in the hopes of scoring perfect answers and finding happiness plus total mutuality will either remain single or end up divorced. Because they know that the reality is this: Marriage IS Built on Surprises, just like Real Life. They also know—and here's a twin irony for you—that we might spend half our marriage trying to prevent those surprises, and the other half trying to resurrect the passion and mystery of surprise that was lost in the process. In both cases, Marriage Enhancement Specialists are here to help, right?

Now, the cultural chasm is so steep here that I get vertigo just thinking about it. Nearly everything about these "ground rules" conspires against the French sensibility. First, there's the tacit assumption that explicitness and practicality create complicity and intimacy. Second, there's a business-oriented approach to love, followed by the somewhat childlike need to have clear instructions for life so that everything will be under control. Then there's the matching assumption that perfect agreement and the ironing out of all emotional, physical, spiritual, and intellectual complexity is even possible, let alone desirable in a relationship.

Before pushing further into this chasm, let's make it clear that there is a difference between rules and protocol. The French might not be fond of rules, but they *are* fond of protocol, and they take it seriously. As British writer Stephen Clarke observed, in France "cutting your lettuce with your fork is punishable by death." When it comes to the protocols of romance, many French women might expect flowers on first "dates" and doors opened for them and dinner bills paid and other forms of gallantry that appear dreadfully unfeminist or old-fashioned ("We are not old-fashioned," my friend Nadine corrected me. "We are traditionalists."). Many of them also find serial dating—or the all-you-can-eat buffet-style Internet dating culture—unappetizing, since there's no actual "romance" to speak of here. There is simply the promise of eternal choice and perpetual dissatisfaction (the lure of someone better eternally beckons in this electronic ecosystem of datable humanity) driven by the wheels of commerce.

French women, of course, are not immune to the promise of instant self-gratification available on the Internet, but there are cultural differences at play that keep things in check. "[When it comes to the Anglo date], both sexes know quite well that when they're 'invited out,' they're one of several names on a list," says French expatriate Cyril. "This is totally banal and accepted; it's even an institution because it doesn't lead to physical relations. Which is, for the French, rather strange. In France, a girl would not accept to compete with three other women; neither would a guy, because the moment you go out with someone, a sexual and exclusive relationship is almost immediately forged and fidelity is automatically set in place even if the relationship is not serious."

A breach of this unspoken social consensus is not a happy moment. If a French woman finds out that she's one of several serial dates, Cyril goes on to say, "The guy would run the risk of getting an enormous slap on his face and never seeing the girl again. In large part that's because of our Latin temperament, which manifests itself through exclusivity and jealousy in a rather particular fashion. We simply test the relationship for a while. If it doesn't work out, we move on to another person." In other words, the French generally "date" the way they eat: one course at a time, preferably hot.

Bottom line: The French generally reject rules designed to legislate or otherwise manage their experience of love and sex. And since the Anglo concept of dating doesn't exist in France, the French aren't barraged with dating secrets, ground rules, dos and don'ts, tips, techniques, and other dating dogma. They're essentially free to do life as they please. How very liberating for them.

We, on the other hand, have rules for meeting men, dating, getting married, getting divorced, getting remarried, getting makeovers, getting dressed, getting organized, getting buff, getting cosmetic surgery. We have rules that, if followed correctly, will help us become a "Creature Unlike Any Other," or a "CUAO" according to a book with the original title: *The Rules.* Ironically, the rules that are supposed to make us happy and "unlike any other"—*Be Yourself!* they chirp—essentially cheerlead us through hoops of friendly fire designed to reengineer ourselves and ultimately shape us not into a CUAO but into a CLEE—or a Creature Like Everyone Else.

Why we choose to outsource our inner lives where the French woman remains warier is a question worth asking. It's also another defining difference between us and the French. We are believers. We believe in advertising and self-help advice and celebrity gossip and compatibility systems and the stern moral rectitude of dos and don'ts. The French, on the other hand, are not believers. They do not believe in following rules or social conventions that are too dogmatic because, like those lane dividers, they see them as an infringement on their individual right to live as they please. That includes some of our most enduring credos, like the Dating Ground Rule #1 wired into our brains from birth: Do Not Sleep with a Man on a First Date or You Will Lose Your Self-respect, Become a Bad Girl, or Burn in Hell for Eternity, whichever comes first. Try that on a French woman. If a French woman wants to sleep with a man the first time they go out—if she feels passion for the man and that passion is mutual—she will. *Pourquoi pas?* It's that simple, even though we'd like to think that it's terribly complex. There is no guilt or shame associated with this. "In France sexuality is neither taboo nor obsessional," writer Michèle Sarde pointed out in an e-mail. "French women assume their sexuality because French society doesn't censor it." That said, though France has its grand tradition of sexual tolerance, French women don't hop into bed like spring rabbits. If French women are discreet, they are also discriminating. Their culture does not sensationalize sex, and neither do they.

We Americans, conversely, do have a tendency to be a wee bit extreme. In fact, we've put the capital in the "E" and turned life into one big Extreme Experience. (See Vestal Virgins on your right and Porn Queens on your left.) Not living with these extremes, nor with the same taboos or rules—not even living, as we'll explore in pages to come, with the enduring fantasy of Happily Ever After—French women have a certain élan vital that was best articulated to me by journalist and social commentator Michèle Fitoussi.

Fitoussi has her finger on the pulse of things *très femme* in France, having written about French women and graced the editorial pages of French *Elle* for decades. We met in her home office in Paris, which was filled with the literary clutter of an indefatigable reader. Fitoussi, looking very French (beauty and brain, little makeup, an air of nonchalant authority that keeps you on your toes), talked about feminism and marriage and other subjects that punctuate the pages of this book, but when I asked her what she considered the single most defining quality of French women, she sat back on a leather couch that nearly dwarfed her small frame and was pensive for a moment; then, with the wail of a siren bebopping in the distance, she replied: "French women have a keen sense of the brevity of time and the immediacy of pleasure."

Touché. In one line Fitoussi defined that mélange of romanticism and realism that seems to linger at the core of all things French. Call it a capacity to seize the moment before it seizes you. Call it a sexy form of existentialism. Call it a realistic awareness of the vagaries and imperfections of real life. French women know that they're not immortal; they don't deny death. No wonder in so many French films death hangs around, nursing a cognac. Let's recall Claude Lelouch's classic *A Man and a Woman*, where both Man (Jean-Louis) and Woman (Anne) are recently widowed. Anne and Jean-Louis meet at their kids' school. Anne hitches a ride back with Jean-Louis after missing her train. There is instant attraction. The presence of death sanctifies the moment. The awareness of mortality fuels their mutual passion, which leads to more road trips, a lot of longing, and absolutely no closure. Rather than death's motivating one to avoid risks in life, the film suggests that not taking emotional risks is a form of death itself.

Sadly, if French women are aware of the brevity of time and the immediacy of pleasure, we Anglos are often too aware of the immediacy of the future and the brevity of pleasure, and part of what keeps that awareness intact is fear. It's tempting to wax on here about the insidious forces in our culture that motivate Americans to be fearful (and thus consume all sorts of dubious and alluring things that will alleviate our fears). I will, however, leave that prickly subject at the side of the road. It often strikes me as interesting, however, that while we Anglos have been relatively unscathed, historically speaking, by many of the calamities that have wreaked havoc in other countries, we live in a culture where threats lurk everywhere, from our fruit bowls and our swimming pools to our public parks and—abundantly—our relationships with other people. In the States I am regularly sent mass e-mails that, when not joking about the lunacy of men, inform me how to avoid abductions in parking lots, track down neighborhood sex offenders, avoid date rape, survive cataclysmic earthquakes, improve my sex life, offset financial ruin, preclude identity theft, prevent viral infections from mutant pathogens, and otherwise manage and control assorted and sundry horrid calamities.

Sometimes just living feels like a liability. In a land like France, however, where truly scary things have threatened millions of people, and revolutions have completely dismantled governments and severed countless heads, making it very difficult to *Have a Nice Day!* and giving people every reason to Be Very Fearful, the French are far more laissez-faire about life than we are. As the old French proverb warns: "He who fears to suffer suffers from fear." The French tend to be contemptuous of precautions and generally don't evade the kind of emotional risks that send us Anglos running—emotional risks that are, let's call a spade a spade, lavishly fed by all those "ground rules" and emotional dos and don'ts. Of course, shit happens, as they say. Love hurts. In fact, it hurts so bad that we get so close to love, yet remain so far from its risks. Nothing, though, is ever quite in our control. "Safe sex, fine," writer Cristina Nehring once opined, "but safe *love* is impossible."

Having a sense of the brevity of time and the immediacy of pleasure certainly helps French women put a relative spin on emotional risks. I'm reminded of the time *Newsweek* infamously declared that a forty-year-old woman "was more likely to be killed by a terrorist" than get married. This declaration sent a generation of single American women into a dating frenzy. (One small step for *Newsweek*, one giant step for the dating service industry.) Two decades later, *Newsweek* admitted that it had been wrong all along, but this time around it dished out new propaganda so far on the opposite end of the spectrum that you could almost hear millions of people in couples therapy and divorce courts scratching their heads. "The real story," *Newsweek* now reported, "is the unexpected happily-ever-afters." Said one interviewee: "I married a fabulous man and I'm crazy about him, and being blissfully married is better than being blissfully single."

Fabulous. Crazy. Blissful. Happily ever after. Helloooo?

Your French woman, were the French media to throw such

a grenade into her love life, would likely dismiss the hype with a big dollop of her trademark realism and question the loony extremes here because, lucky her, she doesn't live in these extremes. Whether it's the menace of having such desperately low chances of marriage that it's time to invest in antiterrorist gear, or the promise of Fabulous-Crazy-Blissful that has all reasonably married people wondering what's wrong with them for not feeling Fabulous-Crazy-Blissful, both predicaments raise the bar to such untenable heights that finding a man or staying with one in sustained ecstasy seems as laborious as having sex while skydiving.

Really, must we be so extreme? Isn't it all so... stressful?

IN HER PREFACE to French *Elle*'s sixty-year anthology, executive editor Valérie Toranian touched on the innate sense of realism and romanticism that beats in the heart of her French sisters: "There are highs and lows. . . . Nothing is written in stone, everything can change. . . . Don't ever give up, even when the boat rocks. That's what gives women their swing: that dance between reality and reverie, with their aspirations that lift them up along with their ten centimeters of high heel to see the world differently. Things vacillate, things sway, things even capsize, but that's life."

Yes, that's life. *C'est la vie. Que sera, sera.* If you're old enough to remember Doris Day crooning that tune, it's probably already lodged in your head.

Who knew that Dorris Day was an existentialist? Though the lyrics were immortalized in Alfred Hitchcock's *The Man Who Knew Too Much*, they could very well be an ode to the French woman's more fatalistic view of love and sex. Might as well make the most of the moment instead of anxiously preparing for (or bracing against) the future, because whatever will be, will be. The future's not ours to see. *Que sera, sera.*

Which leads me to an embarrassing but necessary digression. Long ago, I used to marvel at the smallness of the French purse. It not only seemed commensurate in some way with the smallness of French women, but like the scarf it spoke of an exotic capacity to get by in life with just the essentials. I'd grown up with the notion that purses were practical, so mine was usually filled with paraphernalia for chapped lips, chapped hands, unruly fingernails, allergies, parking lot thugs, dark corners, obscure phone calls, cuts and bruises, multiple hair emergencies, bad weather, bad breath, and bad karma. When I became a mother, list and purse simultaneously ballooned. Nuclear winter might come and go but there'd always be something to combat it in my purse. Eventually, I came to realize that what I was lugging around was not just a lot of useless stuff; I was lugging around the culture of Preparedness.

Now, back when my purse was the size of Mont Blanc, the only thing I didn't seem to carry around with me was a condom—unlike my husband who, when I first met him, when he was working on location in Los Angeles, *did* have condoms stashed in his toiletries case. I knew this because, true confessions, I peered into his toiletry case the first time we met (how low can you possibly get?) and there they were: a bunch of little foiled Trojan squares nestled happily right next to his French toothpaste. Now, condoms—well, that *was* preparedness, but not the kind I was immediately prepared to accept. "Why would he have condoms in his toiletries case," I recall asking of my French friend Anne rather stupidly later that night, "unless he wanted to have sex with the natives?" Anne looked back at me quizzically, then replied. "He is a regular man. That's why. Who were you expecting, Saint Francis of Assisi?"

Clearly, if the French buy into the Culture of Preparedness at all, it's in the interest of being prepared for love and sex, though they're generally less inclined to accept the mental torment associated with the need to be in control—that annoying you-never-knowness which prevents you from living in the moment; that frantic what-if cycle that keeps you forever hinged to a receding future that might never come.

Since this "regular man" was French, he had carte blanche to act, well, French, which meant that he could get away with carrying condoms and drinking Pernod in his bikini bottoms and being sensually dissolute, for all anyone cared. Nobody has an issue about condoms in France, by the way, other than being happy to endorse their frequent use. Condom dispensers are in metro stations for that on-the-go, you-never-know encounter, and every pharmacy features point-of-purchase displays for the same. Even the village where my husband was born—a tiny French hamlet with one church, one bakery, one cow, and lots of senior citizens—often features a gigantic display for condoms in every size, shape, and need in its one and only pharmacy. (The first time I noticed this, I looked at the graying herd around me and wondered: *Who's having all this sex?*) Reaching out to new voters, campaigners for conservative presidential candidate Sarkozy (yes, that's *conservative*) took to the beaches during his election campaign and handed out condoms with the party's logo on them. And on a sweltering August evening in Paris while I was writing this book, Radio France Inter reminded its listeners that people have 50 percent more sex in the summer. "So, folks, don't forget to bring your condoms on vacation," the DJ implored. With this in mind, who could blame Saint Francis of Assisi for carrying condoms in his toiletries case?

Condoms aside, there were bigger problems with this French guy. In short, he broke all of my "ground rules." He was too old. He was too short. He was divorced. He had a kid. He smoked. He actually liked eating blood sausage and listening to Jacques Brel. The list went on. Relationship experts would not approve. When I recited this laundry list to my friend Anne, she stopped me and asked, "But do you *like* him?" When I replied in the affirmative, she simply rolled her eyes and snapped, "Get a life."

- - - - - - - - -

If I'd wanted to play it safe and by the rules, I would have bid this older, smoking, sausage-loving, condom-toting French guy adieu. I had already been to France on the heels of another French man, after all, and I longed to find a truly regular guy who lived in my zip code, or at least in my time zone. But as the days counted down toward his departure and his suggestions that I return to Paris with him became more insistent, a war ensued between the *what if?* and the *why not?* part of my brain. I was well on my way to paralysis-by-analysis when I turned to Anne again. Her advice was as spare and to the point as a French bikini:

ME: What if I go to Paris and it doesn't work out?

ANNE: So? What if that happens? So what? What if you *don't* go? If you don't go, then it doesn't work out, too.

ME: I guess that's one way of looking at it.

ANNE: Of course. You don't go. Nothing happens. So things don't ever work out. This is called "to sabotage life."

ME: Thanks for your vote of confidence.

ANNE: I do not vote for your confidence.

ME: I'm aware of that.

ANNE: Okay, so what if you *do* go and it *does* work out. That would make your love life complicated, no?

ME: Yeah.

ANNE: Well, which do you prefer: a complicated love life or a nonexistent one?

- - - - - - - - -

And so I went. In the blink of an eye ten years passed, I had two children, became a French citizen, learned how to make a really good cheese tart from scratch, and drive around the place de l'Etoile in rush-hour traffic without going into cardiac arrest. Life in France was not without hundreds of complexities, none of which I'd jotted down on my What If list. But this leads me to one last anecdote from those early days when I was packing my bags and saying au revoir to life in the States. I had subleased my dearly beloved rent-controlled apartment by the sea, sold lots and lots of stuff, and packed what I considered the essentials. Among these essentials was a large, old hardcover Pillsbury baking book, which isn't Betty Crocker but is as close as you can get to the same American spirit. It had glossy, four-color photos of every possible baked good known to humankind and an almost biblical authority to it, including nifty conversion charts and measurements that were supposed to make life easier but were in fact positively stupefying in their precision. Also, the book weighed as much as a moose.

Anyhow, when I moved to France, I packed this big American baking book in my bags and took it with me. Now, you may ask, like, *why*? And to that question I would reply, like, I have no idea. Perhaps it was some unconscious longing to hold on to a semblance of America—some atavistic desire for both a symbolic and literal connection to the ebullient goodwill of apple pie. Who knows? Anyhow there it went. And my neighbor in Paris, who lived one floor under us and turned out to be a culinary goddess who only made things from scratch and made fun of my gigantic Pyrex measuring cup (also stashed in my boxes and sent to Paris for equally baffling reasons), was fascinated by this cookbook. It was so instructional. It was so . . . "America!" she said as she leafed through its pages. So much frosting! So many sprinkles! So much happiness! The recipes spoke to a practical, perky, and playful universe unknown to the French. Topsy-Turvy Tropical Muffins. Chocolate Pixies. Jelly Bean Confetti Cake. Ruby Razz Crunch. "How would you translate 'snickerdoodle' and 'cocoa-mallow-cookie-wiche' into French?" Martine asked. "And what *are* they?" To which I replied, like, *je ne sais pas*.

But the most fascinating thing about the book for Martine were all the rules and exact steps and measurements. French women do follow recipes when they cook, of course, but I have just as often seen them improvise and make things from scratch. They make things from scratch and they make them with their hands, not necessarily things you or I might like to make. I once watched Martine devein an entire six-kilo goose liver with her bare hands. It looked very surgical. In any case I have seen her and many of my French friends go to the farmers' market, ask the produce vendor what he/she would recommend for the evening (the vendor having vast encyclopedic knowledge of his or her produce, its particular gastronomic virtues, and the best way to enjoy them), and decide on the spot what to make for that night's dinner party of twelve. This is an act of rule-breaking and risk-taking I put right up

- - - - - - - - -

there with bungee-jumping off the Grand Canyon. You're supposed to *party-plan*, remember? But it is precisely this ability to cook from scratch that I admire, because it speaks not only of culinary flair but also of an ease that comes precisely from a lack of precision; from a joy in the making of, rather than in the joyless utilitarianism of getting things done "right."

My Pillsbury in Paris episode took place, I might add, when Martha Stewart reigned supreme in America. Stewart is not what you'd call a paragon of sensuality or bon vivantism; you could call her, however, an absolute standard of perfection which an untold number of American women have taken very seriously. And it wasn't until I'd stumbled on a passage written by Raoul de Roussy de Sales in his article "Love in America" that I understood why I'd always equated Stewart's love of precision with an uncanny ability to turn pleasure into, well, pain. More important, I understood a connection between cooking and love in America that only became obvious after years of living in France. For its sheer potency, I give you it in its entirety:

The difference between an American cookbook and a French one is that the former is very accurate and the second exceedingly vague. A French recipe seldom tells you how many ounces of butter to use to make crêpes Suzette, or how many spoonfuls of oil should go into a salad dressing. French cookbooks are full of esoteric measurements such as a pinch of pepper, a soupçon of garlic, or a generous sprinkling of brandy. There are constant references to seasoning to taste, as if the recipe were merely intended to give a general direction, relying on the experience and innate art of the cook to make the dish turn out right.

American recipes look like doctors' prescriptions. Perfect cooking seems to depend on perfect dosage. Some of these books give you a table of calories and vitamins—as if that had anything to do with the problem of eating well!

In the same way, there is now flourishing in America a great crop of books which offer precise recipes for the things you should do, or avoid doing, in order to achieve happiness and keep the fires of love at a constant temperature. In a recent issue of *Time* magazine, four such books were reviewed together. Their titles are descriptive enough of the purpose of the authors as well as the state of mind of the readers: Love and Happiness, So You're Going to Get Married, Marriages Are Made at Home, Getting Along Together.

I have not read all these books, but, according to the reviewer, they tend to give practical answers to the same mysterious problem of living with someone of the opposite sex. They try to establish sets of little rules and little tricks which will guarantee marital bliss if carefully followed, in the same way that cookbooks guarantee that you will obtain pumpkin pie if you use the proper ingredients properly measured.

Time's review of these books is very gloomy in its conclusion: "Despite their optimistic tone," it says, "the four volumes give a troubled picture of United States domestic life—a world in which husbands are amorous when wives are not, and vice versa; where conflicts spring up over reading in bed or rumpling the evening paper . . . the whole grim panorama giving the impression that Americans are irritable, aggravated, dissatisfied people for whom marriage is an ordeal that only heroes and heroines can bear."

But I believe that the editors of *Time* would be just as dejected if they were reviewing four volumes about American cooking, and for the same reasons. You cannot possibly feel cheerful when you see the art of love or the art of eating thus reduced to such automatic formulas, even if the experts in these matters are themselves cheerful and optimistic. Good food, the pleasures of love, and those of marriage depend on imponderables, individual taste, and no small amount of luck.

Everything began with an apple and a fig leaf. I'm sure a cookbook followed shortly thereafter. It's been complicated ever since. But if there's one thing that French women know in all this complexity, it's that, to requote Roussy de Sales, the secret of success in love "is to allow for a fairly wide margin of error, and not to forget that human beings are absolutely unable to submit to a uniform rule for any length of time." With that in mind it's not outlandish to suggest that what we Anglos need is not more how-to but more how-*not*-to—how *not* to follow ground rules, lifestyle tactics, and self-help dogma written by people who might not know much more about love and sex than you do and with whom you wouldn't want to experience either. In all due respect.

Nowhere is all this more wickedly obvious than when we tie the conjugal knot in the hopes of living together "happily ever after." Here, yet again, French women bring their own paradoxically practical wisdom to the pursuit of pleasure and the perils of perfection.

HÉLOÏSE: LOVE AT ALL COSTS

The twelfth century was not a particularly swinging time for France. Crusading kingdoms, occasional Viking raids, arranged marriages, free-floating heresy, the frequent wrath of God, bad plumbing, and no e-mail were just some of the inconveniences that plagued the French. Still, it was nearly one thousand years ago that we got one of the most torrid and enduring accounts of romantic love from a French woman who was, in many respects, France's first maiden love child.

Her name was Héloïse. She was a brilliant young scholar who lived in Paris as the ward of her Uncle Fulbert (the name alone spells trouble). At the age of thirteen (or was it seventeen? Or nineteen? Accounts vary; the point is, she was young), Héloïse began to study privately under the tutelage of Peter Abélard, one of the most renowned philosophers and theologians in Paris. And that's when the trouble began.

Héloïse and Abélard relished their mutual academic pursuits, but other passions rustled with undeniable fervor under cloak and tunic. "Her studies allowed us to withdraw in private, as love desired," wrote Abélard of their encounters, "and then with our books open before us, more words of love than of reading passed between us, and more kissing than teaching. My hands strayed more often to her bosom than to the pages; love drew our eyes to look on each other more than reading kept them on our texts."

They were, it turns out, rather nasty. They did it in a refectory on Good Friday. They did it in kitchens and in Uncle Fulbert's boudoir. With Abélard's hands straying more often to her bosom, and Héloïse enjoying every moment of it, teacher and student breached codes of social conduct that would have made tabloid headlines even today. All scruples and sense of propriety disappeared in the heat of their coupling, so keenly did they burn with ardor for each other.

But love and tragedy share a common border. So do biology and sex. In no time Héloïse was pregnant. She gave birth to a son, was exiled to a convent,

- - - - - - - - - -

and secretly married Abélard to save his face. Uncle Fulbert, in a nutshell, was not happy. One night, in what one can only imagine was a big medieval mess, Uncle Fulbert dispatched his henchmen to castrate Abélard. Bereft of his manhood, Abélard retreated to a monastery, where he became a monk.

When Abélard lost his family jewels, he found God and renounced his former passions with Héloïse as sinful, their love as lust. But if Abélard was now a eunuch, it was Héloïse who had balls. "I would have had no hesitation, God knows, in following you or going ahead at your bidding to the flames of hell," she wrote to Abélard in love letters that remain among the most famous in the Western world. Héloïse was not only ready to sacrifice her Frequent Flyer miles to heaven for the passion still beating in her bosom; she was ready to renounce all forms of compensatory material gains (Material Girl—*Not*) as hell on earth. "If Augustus, emperor of the whole world, saw fit to honor me with marriage and conferred all the earth on me to possess forever, it would be dearer and more honorable to me to be called, not his empress, but your whore."

Neither religious exile nor the strident moral dogma of her time kept her from expressing her libidinous longings, and her unwillingness to conform to social conventions had a distinctly contemporary French bite to it. "Even during the celebration of the Mass, when our prayers should be purer, lewd visions of those pleasures take such a hold upon my unhappy soul that my thoughts are on their wantonness instead of on prayers," she wrote. "I should be groaning over the sins I have committed, but I can only sigh for what I have lost."

In the end, Abélard remained deeply connected to Héloïse, and it was he who requested that they be buried together. (They are, in the Père Lachaise cemetery.) Both of them became romantic martyrs and icons. When a flurry of books about Héloïse and Abélard was published a few years ago, Cristina Nehring opined in *The New York Times* that in her rejection of social conventions—in her unwillingness to equate love with marriage, money, or moral dogma—Héloïse was "at once intrepid and idealistic, transgressive and submissive, taboo-busting and sweet-natured, noble and naughty." In other words, in her ownership of her amorous desires, in her breaking of rules and not giving a damn, Héloïse was one thoroughly modern French girl.

Four

PERFECTION

On the perils of exalted standards of happiness and moral perfection, the virtues of agreeing to disagree, the reason why Emma Bovary is the ultimate Desperate Housewife, and other discomfort zones both large and small

That the relationship between men and women offers a wide scale of variations seldom occurs to the experts. It is not necessarily true that there is but one form of love worth bothering about, and that if you cannot get the deluxe model, with a life guarantee of perfect functioning, nothing else is worthwhile. It is not true either that you can indefinitely pursue the same quest for perfection.

—RAOUL DE ROUSSY DE SALES

Happiness is poor preparation for human contact.

—COLETTE

Here's a typical American joke that you won't hear in France: One evening, Jenny arrived home from work to find the children bathed, one load of clothes in the washer and another in the dryer, dinner on the stove, and the table set. She was astonished—something's up. It turns out that her husband, Ralph, had read an article that said wives who worked full-time and had to do their own housework were too tired to have sex. The night went well, and the next day she told her office friends all about it.

> "We had a great dinner. Ralph even cleaned up. He helped the kids do their homework, folded all the laundry, and put everything away. I really enjoyed the evening."
>
> "But what about afterward?" asked her friends.
>
> "Oh, that was perfect, too. Ralph was too tired to have sex. . . ."
>
> God is good.

God may be good, but is sex with our husbands really that bad? Taking our cues from the zeitgeist at large, the response would have to be yes. Forget about *Sex and the City* and think of the more sobering life of *Everybody Loves Raymond*, where great trails of marital disgruntlement must be forged in order to have sex.

To a French woman, this predicament is woeful and Jenny's joke is not funny.

"What does God have to do with it?" my friend Nadine asked.

"It's just a way of expressing gratitude," I replied.

"For what?"

"For keeping our husbands from wanting to sleep with us."

She looked back at me in silent disapproval.

In the French version of the same joke (if it even existed), Jenny's friends would have sent her to a weekend hydrotherapy retreat and told her to get a grip.

One of the pitfalls in entering this conjugal wilderness is the assumption that French women don't have similar disgruntlements as Anglo women. Of course the marital den is a universally problematic place, filled with scary, entangled gardens that must be regularly pruned or systematically bushwhacked. That said, while American-style lamentations have begun to make an appearance on the French stage—the majority of French women work, after all—they haven't reached the strident Sturm und Drang of the Anglo way of life, nor are they fraught with the same guilt-ridden mommy madness. When *Desperate Housewives* debuted on French TV, I asked a journalist why the title hadn't been translated into French. His response: "Because there's no such thing in France." On its success in France, my friend Karine suggests: "It's campy and exotic for the French. We recognize it as an exaggerated portrait of neurotic women written by homosexuals. Don't Americans?" *Don't they?*

Journalist Corine Goldberger framed it differently in the French edition of *Marie Claire*: "Americans hooked on *Sex and the City* are now passionate about the depressing life of four chic suburbanites." Describing the sexual frustrations and "mommy madness" of the desperate American wife, Goldberger asked: "Will France experience the same phenomenon? For the moment, we're not there."

With this in mind, let us push on. We have already explored a few gray zones. Let us now explore a few discomfort zones.

Marriage is obsolete and a trap.

—CATHERINE DENEUVE

Only homosexuals and priests want to get married.

—LOUISE DE VILMORIN,
FRENCH WRITER/JOURNALIST

Life experience and socioanthropological reporting from the French front lines yields these observations: The institution of marriage is not an institution in France at all. It's a "soft revolution," to quote sociologists, which has the French bucking the social and religious trappings of traditional marriage for a different kind of coupledom. Despite occasional blips on the nuptial radar (and, yes, you will find them), more than 50 percent of French women choose cohabitation over marriage. Even when little *bébé* comes into the picture (cohabitation hasn't stopped French women from having babies at a healthy clip), you won't see French bridezillas scrambling for a prenup agreement or rushing to City Hall to tie the knot.

In this regard it seems we Anglos and the French are moving away from one another like those galaxies drifting off into space: Where we increasingly embrace the institution of marriage (the bling, the ring, the wedding planners—the whole baronial business of it), the French increasingly question its social conventions at its core. Where we turn to various religious and self-help communities for a sense of matrimonial morality, with "marriage-education organizations" and even a National Institute of Relationship Enhancement, the French are increasingly cynical about any predetermined doctrines espoused by the Church or any other established organization. Where we publicize traditional marriage as a celebration and sign of social status, many French see the custom as part of a bourgeois culture with dusty, provincial overtones.

In fact, among the many French couples I know, I'm not sure who's officially married and who's not—and the idea of clarifying that point would seem strangely irrelevant to them. It just doesn't matter to the French the way it does, profoundly so, to Anglos, because as France Prioux, director at INED (Institut National d'Etudes Démographiques), once explained: "There is a certain revolt in France against established institutions. This is part of the French nature, the French spirit. There is no social disapproval in France with not being married. This is the case across the entire socioeconomic spectrum. People now ask: 'Why marry?'"

Why, indeed?

Of course, the French still get married in big traditional church weddings with all the trimmings. They also adore the large three-day wedding in one's country home that often ends in joyful debauchery. And, yes, there are bridal businesses and wedding planners in France just as, in the tradition of our big free-market global economy, there are McDonald's and reality TV shows and other forms of commercial biomass growing in even the remotest corners of the planet. But the majority of French women aren't rushing to the altar, and this should come as no surprise to mainstream America ever since French presidential candidate Ségolène Royal caused a stir in this country for her unorthodox (to us) but extremely common (to the French) marital status.

If the French tend to "revolt" against the established institution of marriage, they are equally cynical about the symbols and myths that go along with it—most notably, the enduring belief in the Happily Ever After. And here we part

- - - - - - - - - -

company even more firmly with the French. Americans are, needless to say, terrifically obsessed with weddings and marriage. We invest staggering sums of money and energy into the Big Moment, and then we invest equally staggering sums to make sure that all subsequent moments last till death us do part. Of course, they rarely do—at least not without a bit of turbulence once we've reached cruising altitude.

In fact it seems that some get cold feet before they even leave the runway. According to a recent marriage study the seven-year itch is actually a three-year itch. This itch is so, well, itchy that as one researcher told *The New York Times*, "Some folks start getting less happy at the wedding reception." Talk about the law of diminishing returns. Marriage seems a little like the universe: it starts with a Big Bang, then it drifts away from itself toward the scary suburbs of outer space. None of this stops us, however, from feverishly investing in the business of marriage, primarily because if the pursuit of happiness is written into our Declaration of Independence, the pursuit of the Happy Ending is most certainly written into our culture.

Now you can't argue with happiness. Happiness is good. Happiness is American. Happiness is so wrapped up in our national identity and sense of ourselves that being unhappy seems almost unpatriotic. Edith Wharton once suggested that what Americans all long for is "a tragedy with a happy ending." Americans love the raging Tony Sopranos and the dysfunctional cohorts buried Six Feet Under, but when sadness slips into the cracks of our own souls, the imperative to remain "happy" bears down on us like a two-by-four.

Americans invented the Happy Face. The French invented Existentialism. Need we say more? In fact, when I grew up, the Happy Face was the civic leitmotif. The whole world was going to hell in a handbasket but the US was still dancing away to Bobby McFerrin's hit song "Don't Worry, Be Happy!" At the time, I actually tried very hard not to worry and be happy (which, as we all know, has the annoying inverse effect of making you worry endlessly). I was a bookish brunette who hung out with similar charming misfits, and together we were tyrannized by cheerleaders, prom girls, and other members of the Mean Girl Ruling Class because we didn't fit in. Like all good girls we tried hard to stuff any little wads of crumpled discontent into our pockets and put a smile on our face, but the harder we tried, the weirder we actually felt (and looked). When young adulthood finally bloomed, we stumbled on Sartre. *L'enfer, c'est les autres!* he declared, or "Hell is other people." We couldn't have agreed more.

No wonder we were suddenly enchanted by French women. Not only were these women a sensual and resilient counterpart to the one-size-fits-all beauty standard advocated around us—they weren't cookie-cutter pretty but they had that maddening French capacity to transform quirky particularities, even ugliness, into compelling sexiness. More important, they seemed to make an art form out of ennui. There was a certain romance to their melancholy, and as they clung to the arms of men in their strange hats and wicked shoes, they were a refreshing reprieve from the relentless Happy Face-ism around us. In fact, their enigmatic sophistication seemed all wrapped up in the way they diverged from the aggressively sunny imperatives of "happy."

Having grown up with this French sensibility, author Véronique Vienne recalled how she had to work hard to adapt to the mandated cheerfulness of American culture when she moved from France to the States; she practiced her smile in the mirror, trying her best to look like "Miss Congeniality," before concluding that "in this country, the obligation we feel to conform to exalted standards of happiness can be pure misery." It is also Vienne who brings us the pertinent observation that "happiness" for an American is actually considered "joie de vivre" for the French—or as Vienne describes it, "a form of bliss triggered by the world at large, not by an internal reality. Unlike happiness, which can be described as an inner state of contentment, joie de vivre is not self-involved. You derive this kind of joy from acknowledging greatness outside yourself—in things, in nature, in others."

Like that infinite gamut of romance, joie de vivre sprawls along an infinite gamut of emotions; for the French, joie de vivre is, according to Vienne, "a kind of lighthearted but existential deportment that is separate from—and doesn't interfere with—their brooding. In the French mind, happy and sad are not mutually exclusive emotions; gloom and glee can coexist peacefully." (I'm reminded of a scene in Jean-Luc Godard's *Breathless*, when Patricia—American actress Jean Seberg, famous for having a short pixie cut back when the word "bouffant" really meant something—declares: "I don't know if I'm free because I'm sad or if I'm sad because I'm free.")

It's in accepting perfectly imperfect human emotions, with a certain realistic snap to her gait, that the French woman goes into marriage (if she goes into it at all, that is). And because she doesn't live with the enduring belief in Happily Ever After, the French woman also doesn't live under the shadow of its biggest mascot: the princess.

There's no denying that as the largest girl franchise on the planet, the princess is nothing if not spectacular in America. It's equally hard to deny the *sagesse* in the observations of Peggy Orenstein, who once opined in a *New York Times* piece ("What's Wrong with Cinderella?") that beyond the happy pink patina something cruel and unhappy looms. "There are no studies proving that playing princess directly damages girls' self-esteem," she writes. "But there is evidence that young women who hold the most conventionally feminine beliefs—who avoid conflict and think they should be perpetually nice and pretty—are more likely to be depressed." (Orenstein goes on to describe that emotional axis of evil that ensnares the princess in the "paralyzing pressure to be 'perfect' . . . not only to get straight A's and be the student-body president, editor of the newspaper, and captain of the swim

- - - - - - - - -

team but also to be 'kind and caring,' 'please everyone, be very thin and dress right.' ")

French girls grow up with their princesses, too, of course, but somewhere along the line they end up not wanting to *be* them. Let's recall that the French have had their share of real princesses and evil queens. They also had a revolution, the discreet charm of the bourgeoisie no longer seemed so charming, and Marie Antoinette's head ended up in a basket. Not only do they tend to scorn icons of princessly perfection; they were done with the fairy tale of the princess itself long ago. They knew that a fairy-tale wedding with horse-drawn carriage and all the trimmings couldn't even help Lady Di and her prince avoid all that "pure misery," because for the French a hint of tragedy, or at least multipurpose tribulation, laces any vision of absolute perfection or happiness. I'm reminded of the time my French girlfriend Marie-Louise first stumbled on the wedding announcements in *The New York Times*. Scanning each photo with a critical eye, one brow raised like a dangling apostrophe, she commented rather dryly: "The only time you see announcements published like this in France is if royalty married, or if you are in a tiny village where everyone knows everyone else and the butcher's daughter is marrying the mayor's son. America is like one big European province."

Well, maybe so; still, that doesn't make those wedding announcements any less fascinating. "The straight woman's sports pages" is how Carrie Bradshaw described them in

Sex and the City, and she got it right. We may read them out of sheer curiosity, peppered with sprinkles of envy (this is how your life *could* have been, if only you'd had the right social pedigree). Or we may read them for the lush perversion of wondering, despite the perfect happiness that radiates from each photo, when these couples might unravel at the seams, because if we're interested in the thrill of victory, we're equally compelled by the agony of defeat that hangs, implicitly and inevitably, behind any image of perfection.

For the French, marriage does not belong in the world of Happily Ever After; rather, it belongs squarely in the middle of real life, with all its complexities and contradictions, its tensions, compromises, and unresolved longings. It is something to enter carefully, even warily, if at all, without forgetting that marriage is an emotional contract, not a business contract, that it generally *is* built on surprises.

In fact, it's often precisely the quest for perfection that leads one down a path toward imperfection by raising the bar to impossible heights. As our journalist friend De Roussy de Sales observed yet again, this is a particularly American obsession. "The American woman entertains the delightful illusion that there must be some man on this earth who can understand her," he writes. "[She] does not want to be understood for the mere fun of it. What she actually wishes is to be helped to solve certain difficulties which, in her judgment, impede the successful development of her inner self. She seldom accepts the idea that maladjustments and misunderstandings are not only normal but bearable once you have made up your mind that, whatever may be the ultimate aim of our earthly existence, perfect happiness through love or any other form of expression is not part of the program."

Which is another way of saying what my friend Sylvie said: "Perfection is not expected in France. The French are too realistic for that. Our mothers will tell us that nothing is perfect; that human nature is imperfect and that relationships are about learning to compromise." They will also tell their French daughters that if something looks too good to be true, it probably is. French writer/editor Michèle Fitoussi echoes that sentiment. "When you speak of the 'perfect couple' to a French person, they're immediately going to look for a crack in the asphalt—for the fault line. We're going to wonder if the husband is gay, if the woman has a lover, if they both have lovers. We know that disputes are okay for a couple . . . disputes relieve pressure. They're natural; they actually help. Sometimes a huge dispute can reinforce a couple. French women aren't afraid of this." In lieu of rushing off to couples therapy when feelings flare up ("No, no!" Fitoussi is quick to retort when I run this option past her), French people "often make up under the covers. You reconcile things in the intimacy of your bedroom and, voilà, you move on."

Not all French couples kiss and make up with such boudoir nonchalance, of course, but in matters of the heart

French women do tend to be less afraid of strong messy feelings and passions. A bitter marital spat doesn't imply to the French that anything is necessarily wrong or imperfect and therefore needs fixing, or that it's time to ditch your mate and move on to a new one and thus undermine that tight hot knot of the French family unit. No, the French find more . . . *creative* ways of dealing with that. (More on this imminently.) In *Mariage, Sexe et Tradition* Pascale Wattier and Olivier Picard suggest that even while marital disputes might provoke hatred, they're also moments of truth; these "healthy storms" are preferable to the parched desert of an empty marriage because, as Wattier and Picard suggest to their French readers, "a couple that doesn't have marital disputes is a couple that's stuck—a couple that isn't evolving."

I used to be awed by the French capacity to argue and lock horns, only to shrug things off without harboring long-standing resentments. I later came to realize that it's not so much an uncanny French nonchalance at play here; rather, it's a willingness to accept and even enjoy the fact that locking horns and rutting around is as natural to humans as it is to wildebeests. The French basically agree to disagree. In fact, they *like* to disagree. It's a sign of intelligence and passion. It's a sign that one has opinions, which, we'll remind you, is a *good* thing in France. Allowing those opinions to snap, crackle, and pop over an open fire is not only a perfectly reasonable expression of passion; it is far more compelling than the flat line of mutual consensus. As Montaigne once put it: "There is no conversation more boring than the one where everyone agrees."

Now "relationship experts" in America might lead us to believe that a couple without marital disputes is, indeed, a perfect couple. It might even be a couple that has mastered the Practical Application of Intimate Relationship Skills—or one of those perfect PAIRS! But it's precisely this inclination to seek harmony at all costs, even to the point of leveling idiosyncrasies and imperfections (or "fixing" them), that French academician Raymonde Carroll takes to task in her book *Cultural Misunderstandings: The French-American Experience*. This handy manifesto is a perennial hit on the underground expatriate must-read list because of its insightful dual perspective about Franco-American relations. It doesn't take much to see that Carroll sits squarely with her compatriot Montaigne. "I would go so far as to say that one [a French person] would probably be wary of a couple who always seemed to be in perfect agreement," she writes. "People would probably begin to worry and suspect that there was 'something wrong,' that 'something was fishy.' And in the end one might even be somewhat sickened by their being (or having become) 'rather boring.'"

Rather boring. The kiss of death in France.

Carroll takes this ball and runs the distance with it, suggesting that the ideal Anglo couple "always agrees. No contradictions, no admonition, no intervention, no advice, no disagreement, no radically different opinions, no fighting, no frowns, no disapproving silences, no reproaches, and especially, especially, no yelling. All conflict, all threat of conflict or suggestion of conflict, is a bad sign: The couple has 'problems' and probably will not last. But the absence of conflict is not enough: there has to be manifest support of the other, which must be constantly reaffirmed."

When this support is not reaffirmed—or when our cultural bias for good sportsmanship, team playing, and Ultimate Partnership is compromised by our spouse (and it will be, because, remember, Marriage *Is* Built on Surprises)—things get a little dicey, no matter which culture you live in. Sometimes the imperfections of marriage will drive humans, among the most imperfect life-forms on earth, after all, to roam the open prairies for what the French euphemistically call "parallel lives," "contingent relationships," or simply "adventures." As Alexandre Dumas suggested, "The chain of wedlock is so heavy that it takes two to carry it, sometimes three." American author Laura Kipnis put it more succinctly: "Adultery is one way of protesting the confines of married life. Of course, there's always murder."

> *I used to be Snow White, but I drifted.*
>
> —MAE WEST, HONORARY FRENCH GIRL

Let's get one enduring perception/reality problem out of the way right now. PERCEPTION: the French are all adulterous. Everyone has, is, knows, or wants to be a mistress. REALITY:

according to an exhaustive study comparing the sexuality of Americans and the French, Americans are actually more adulterous than the French. "The difference between France and the States is that in France the extramarital partner lasts a long time, whereas in the States it's often a one-night stand," summarized research director Alain Giami. "We've noticed that Americans have more of them [affairs], in shorter duration, than the French. The major difference between French women and American women can be summarized as follows: the French are marathoners, and Americans are sprinters."

In other words we all push the marital envelope, we just wear different running shoes.

Of course we never look at it that way. On the one hand, French history is so densely packed with tales of parallel lives and *liaisons dangereuses* that are so intimately woven into its cultural heritage, that to whip up a polemic around the subject would be banal by French standards. On the other hand, we Anglos are convinced that we have the monopoly on moral values, even though it's often the biggest moral pontificators among us who literally get caught with their pants down.

The relationship between love and marriage is a relatively recent one, lest we forget. Love, with all its voluptuous tentacles, often found its place outside the confines of conjugal life. Volumes have been written about French courtesans who've seduced and serviced men of all ranks; more contemporarily, French literature and cinema have brought to America a world where innumerable affairs within affairs are nestled like Russian dolls in snug, libidinous stacks. If you take all this at face value (and unless you live in France, how can you not?), everyone is fooling around with somebody else's husband, brother, father, uncle, neighbor, plumber, car mechanic, accountant, or music teacher. The French, it seems, just can't take their hands off each other's spouses.

In the real world, adultery creates pyrotechnics in French relationships, like it does in other relationships, and it's one of the top reasons for divorce in France. Not all French men and women are happily passing off their spouses while they shrug away the tribulations of conjugal life with a cruel and jaunty *c'est la vie*. That said, the French are more at ease with the notion that one single person can't easily satisfy a lifetime of personal desire, and they're fascinated by infidelities as a prism through which to explore this wild terrain of the human heart. There is little American-style fire and brimstone in French film, where lovers pay the price of pleasure with their lives in freakish fashion. Recall the hapless French—ahem!—lover in *Unfaithful* who ends up wrapped in a carpet and thrown in a trash heap, or Glenn Close's demonic bunny-in-the-boiler breakdown and subsequent bathtub demise in *Fatal Attraction*.

When death comes to the French adulterer or to the "adulterated"—as it often does; fooling around can be fatal even if you're French—it's frequently strangely peaceful; a poignant and fatalistic ceding to life's unruly passions and injustices, tinged with the buttery hues of tragic longing. In *Jules and Jim*, Catherine (Jeanne Moreau) calmly drives a car off a bridge with Jim in tow, thus putting an end to one of cinema's most idyllic ménages à trois. Upon hearing of her husband's affair, the deceived wife in Agnès Varda's *Le Bonheur* looks at her spouse with a melancholy regard that is almost sensual in its remorse, then quietly demurs and drowns herself in a lake. Death, for the French, comes with a certain flourish.

For centuries French literature has also brimmed with stories of tangled and torrid ardor, but for many of these literary libertines infidelity is presented as a transgressive force with the power to illuminate the emotional thickets of human existence itself, not just a fabulous way to have more sex. When it comes to family values—to the challenge of keeping that tight hot nut of the family unit intact—many French women cultivate their secret gardens elsewhere precisely *in* the interest of family values. "Paradox?" *L'Express* asked its readers in a recent headline about this phenomenon: "While the French staunchly advocate family happiness, never has the issue of sexual freedom within the couple been so questioned." No, never *has* it been so front and center for the French. If Anglos seem preoccupied with the sexless marriage, the French would seem equally preoccupied with adultery.

"Elastic when it comes to their initial commitments, the French are becoming increasingly pragmatic," note Pascale

Wattier and Olivier Picard. "They defend each couple's right to redefine their own marital freedom in a subtle balance between the secret and the transparent."

Philosopher Patricia Delahaie similarly reports in her book *Fidèle, pas fidèle?* (Faithful, Unfaithful?) that while fidelity remains a sacred value for the French, they are willing to "yield more readily" to the idea of infidelity. "A lover is all about personal development and a lot less expensive than a shrink!" one woman declares in Delahaie's book. Pragmatic, indeed.

Taking vows, of course, never stopped anyone from being unfaithful, though it does tend to make it more difficult to engage in rationalizations once you've gone the distance. Better, then, to just keep things to yourself, so French thinking goes, and cultivate your secret garden in the privacy of your own despair and longing. In his *Adultères* (Adultery) eminent French pediatrician Aldo Naouri lambastes the extramarital tryst (yes, there *are* a few lone detractors in this busy French Home Gardening Center), but when pushed by an interviewer, he concedes that if adultery actually allowed a woman to sustain her marriage and thus keep her family intact, he'd be the first to green-light the affair. "My advice would be, 'Follow your passion, don't tell anyone about it, and see what happens.' If adultery actually allows one to preserve their marriage, I'd say, 'Do it!'"

And French women *are* doing it—or at least they're increasingly comfortable with the idea that adultery need not always be a slash-and-burn operation that leaves smoldering debris in its wake; that, with the right amount of discretion (presumably, a heaping dose of it), "parallel lives" might possibly help sustain a marriage. This radical notion was put forth to much controversy in a French *Elle* essay by Caroline Rochman. "Adultery should be used like potion, uniquely with parsimony," she wrote." Well dosed, it heals; overdosed, it knocks you out."

Decades earlier, Edith Wharton had explored how the French manage to honor family infrastructures while providing a unique exception for extracurricular love. It is, Wharton wrote, "not because love is thought unimportant, but on account of its very importance, and of the fact that it is not conceivably to be fitted into any stable association between man and women. It is because the French have refused to cut love in two that they have not attempted to subordinate it to the organization of the family." In acknowledging the fact that love "moves to a different rhythm, and keeps different seasons," the French are better equipped to "frankly recognize its right to its own place in life." Wharton refers to this place as "the poetry of life." In her discreet fashion she does not use the word "adultery." We know, however, exactly what she's talking about.

It's a long-standing European position to presume that the "poetry of life" can be accepted if it helps sustain a family and a marriage, and this doesn't always imply that mutual deception is required (though in most cases, it certainly can't hurt). You'd be hard-pressed to find a French person who doesn't know at least one individual with a long-standing lover whose presence is no secret. Nor is it uncommon to find a certain type of older French man whose wife has accepted with almost condescending nonchalance a mistress of many years. (Mitterrand immediately comes to mind.) You also get a smattering of open marriages and other postmodern living arrangements that support the idea of personal space as a necessary ingredient in that mysterious recipe of enduring love. Says Janine, who is married but lives in an adjoining apartment from her husband: "There is nothing more anxiety-producing than intimacy. People think that by sharing everything—every little detail, every experience—you become intimate. But, no. This is grotesque. This is deeply and profoundly stressful. Human beings do not thrive in such stifling daily proximity. Look at urban density. Look at how it is emotionally draining. People think our arrangement detracts value from our relationship but in fact it enhances it!"

All things being equal, the French are particularly adept at adapting the vagaries of the heart to the imperatives of the real world without excessive moral hand-wringing. They're equally adept at framing these imperatives in a philosophical light, even when things get a bit racy. In *Il n'est jamais trop tard pour aimer plusieurs hommes* (It's Never Too Late to Love Several Men), Françoise Simpère depicts her thirty-year open marriage with its multiple lovers as "rather unusual, anticonformist even, because it escaped the classic model of conjugal life." But it's interesting to note that in its nonconformity her marriage was, for Simpère at least, "an existence that conforms to what life is actually all about: unexpected, sometimes difficult, strewn with both traps and real joys." Describing these traps and joys, Simpère concedes that living outside the box hasn't always been simple, but it provided "the beginning of a sort of response to the metaphysical question about the meaning of existence."

No French woman managed to explore simultaneously the "meaning of existence" and the nature of open marriages better than the High Priestess of Existentialism herself. Of all the *liaisons dangereuses* that have gone down in history, the adventures of de Beauvoir and Sartre in the Being and Nothingness of Coupledom shine with a certain grandiosity in the French firmament. Simone de Beauvoir and Jean-Paul Sartre famously made a "pact" to have an open relationship with full disclosure of all encounters. The ensuing debauchery and emotional tribulations have been well documented, and the jury is still out, decades later, on whether the whole arrangement was good or not. Françoise Giroud saw in their iconoclasm a coupling that allowed both of them "to preserve a love, a tenderness, a reciprocal respect, a living, demanding relationship, what was actually steadfast fidelity. What bound them to each other proved to be indestructible. Is that exceptional? More enviable than the continual pursuit of passion interspersed with divorces? Oddly enough, this man and woman who rejected marriage ended up having a successful . . . marriage." Others have not been so quick to exalt this iconoclastic arrangement.

Whatever the case may be, de Beauvoir and Sartre certainly kicked down the door of the traditional conjugal model. When it came to infidelity and her particular "arrangement," de Beauvoir was unapologetic. "We were two of a kind," she wrote of herself and Sartre, "and our relationship would endure as long as we did: but it could not make up entirely for the fleeting riches to be had from encounters with different people. I wish that every human life might be pure, transparent freedom," she once wrote. Like pieces from a blast that still contain the remnants of its initial conflagration, this message of personal and sexual freedom was blown by the winds of social change in France and continues to infuse the *air du temps*.

With their more tolerant and elastic view of marriage comes the social consensus among the French that in the wilderness of love, secret gardens are bound to grow with all their enticing tendrils. Managing and pruning this perilous horticulture often involves a set of life skills that you can't get in a lifestyle handbook. If you're going to have a secret garden, it certainly helps to be a grown-up. Let's not forget that when you break down the word "adultery," you get its most important component part: the word "adult."

If there's any consistent Frenchness in all this, it would have to be in the French woman's capacity to assume certain passions despite the social constraints of marriage. And, indeed, when it comes to breaking the codes of the bourgeoisie—to kissing social conventions good-bye in the name of personal pleasures, passions or . . . desperate longing—there's nothing like adultery. Ironically enough, members of the bourgeoisie have always enjoyed this "discreet charm" and are often among its most ardent practitioners. Who better to exemplify this phenomenon for us all than the ultimate French bourgeois adulteress—Emma Bovary?

Emma was one big unhappy French package, and if her woe endures today, it's in large measure because her predicament as the ultimate Desperate Housewife—her longings, her spirit crushed by the dreary constraints of conjugal life, her soulful sense that a more expansive passion exists outside the box of marriage—is a universal one. Playing one side against the other, Emma's lover, Rudolph, pins the tail on the donkey when, in a ruse to seduce Emma, he declares: "Ah, but there are two moralities: The petty, conventional morality, the morality of men, which is constantly changing and which makes such a loud noise, floundering about on the earth like this collection of imbeciles you see before you. But the other, the eternal morality, is all around us and above us like the countryside that surrounds us and the blue sky that sends down its light."

Floundering around with a collection of imbeciles or enjoying eternal morality in the light-filled countryside—frankly, which would *you* choose?

Balancing between a life of deadening domesticity and

delicious disgrace, Emma eventually "steps into the light," but when she enters that "marvelous realm in which everything would be passion, ecstasy, and rapture," we know it's too good to be true. If we continue to be fascinated by Emma Bovary, it's perhaps because on some level we've become a nation of postmodern Emma Bovarys ourselves, struggling with those "two moralities" and their problematic seductions.

Yet again Edith Wharton perfectly frames adultery as it hangs on the domestic mantelpiece in France when she writes that love "is too grave a matter for boys and girls, and not grave enough to form the basis of marriage; but in the relations between grown people, apart from their permanent ties (and in the deepest consciousness of the French, marriage still remains indissoluble), they allow it, frankly and amply, the part it furtively and shabbily, but no less ubiquitously, plays in Puritan societies."

"INDIVIDUALS AREN'T RESPONSIBLE for the failure of marriage," Simone de Beauvoir once said." It's the institution itself that is the problem." De Beauvoir was no pillar of traditional marital stability, but she was exceptionally French in her refusal to let social conventions hijack her sense of personal freedom, laced as it was with her own brand of high-octane existentialism. The more you try to pen in their sense of personal freedom, the more likely the French

----

are to kick the barn door open, precisely because our mutinous French friends aren't fond of established institutions (except, for just cause, the ones that secure their beloved social benefits).

Just as French women generally don't strive for exalted standards of happiness, neither do they strive for exalted standards of moral perfection. And if exalted standards of happiness and moral perfection aren't high on the French woman's agenda, it's because the inherent futility of both has been ingrained in her culture for centuries. The big problem with perfection is that it's rarely perfect. Ditto for exalted standards of happiness, which generally don't stay exalted for long. Reality has a way of creeping into even the best-laid plans.

What we Anglos often perceive as perfection in French women—the perfect table setting, the perfect sense of style, the perfect meal—is often more a form of aesthetics (from where we get *l'art de table*, *l'art de vivre*). In fact, French women not only have a certain latitude for the kind of imperfections that we Americans tend to take on as home, spouse, or self-improvement projects; they have a way of accepting those imperfections as part of human nature and Mother Nature—and deriving pleasure from both.

ON THE BEAUTY OF NOT
GIVING A DAMN

One thing you have to give up is attaching impor-
tance to what people see in you.

—JEANNE MOREAU

American women don't know many things about
themselves. They try to be right. You have to be
yourself. But you have to know who you are.

—SONIA RYKIEL

French women, generally speaking, know who they
are. In fact, their sense of self-possession slices the
air with such enviable sharpness that they often
don't seem to give a damn what we think of them.
News flash: they don't. That's partly why there's such
an idiosyncratic edge to their beauty, their style, and
their (I am loath to use the clichéd term again but
here I go) je ne sais quoi. French women aren't overly
concerned with trying to be right. More important,
they don't grow up with the cultural mandate to be
liked. In Stephen Clarke's novel *A Year in the Merde*,
a hapless Brit learns this lesson the hard way when
he tries to fumble his way into French hearts, to
no avail: "I was witnessing an important lesson in

Parisian life. I mustn't try to make people like me. That's much too English. You've got to show them you don't give a shit what they think. Only then will you get what you want. I'd been doing it all wrong, trying to win people over. If you smile too much, they think you're retarded."

Yes, it's true. They'll think you're retarded. Or Anglo-Saxon. Because they don't give a damn about being liked. And we do.

This singular difference between Anglos and the French is tangled up in the cruel, tender machinations of youth. For one of the first pressures that bear down on Anglo girls is the pressure not only to be liked but to be *like* everyone else. This initial feat of self-transformation often involves loosening one's grip on that quiet sense of inner self and hitching one's wagon to a single standard of beauty. The stress of leaping through that hoop insinuates itself into the young heart and soul with a vengeance, and insecurities go from being hard little buds of confusion to over-ripe, snarled, and tyrannical fruits that hang on the vine as we age.

In France the cultural norms wired into the French brain at an early age are almost exactly the opposite. Says Nicole: "In the U.S. you have to fit a certain norm to be perceived as beautiful, to feel like you're somebody. And everyone tries to follow that norm. In France, it's just the opposite. For French women, if you don't fit a standard mold, you're more compelling. If you don't look like everyone else— if you express something different or somehow unique—you're interesting, you're special, and that makes you attractive and sexy."

For Anglo girls when being liked isn't wrapped up in the conventions of being a good girl—in pleasing others, in being "perfect" or "right"—it's often bound up in the mandate to be popular. Being "popular," on the other hand, has no place in the hierarchy of girlhood preoccupations in France because, like the training bra or relationship enhancement workshops, there's no concept for it. "It took me a long time living in America to understand this notion of popularity that obsesses Americans," adds Nicole. "What does this mean, 'to be popular,' I would ask myself? I realized that it means that you are liked by everybody, which means that in some way you correspond to everybody. This concept does not exist in France because there is no desire to be liked by everyone in our culture. On the contrary, if you are liked by everyone it suggests that you are somehow bland. There is nothing authentic or original about you, never mind sexy." Alexis de Gemini, who had the peculiar idea of producing a French version of the American show *The Bachelor* for French TV (called—*très* original!—*Le Bachelor*), emphasized this heretical aspect of French women when I asked him to describe the most outstanding difference between single American women and their French counterparts. His response: "American women have a natural talent to act like they're natural; this is something you Americans grow up learning how to do. French women are just the opposite. They appreciate conflict and don't give a shit what you think of them. There's a strong tendency not to be liked but to like who you are and try to show that."

Nothing wrong with wanting to be liked, of course. This cheerful national trait makes Americans among the most civic-minded and friendliest people on the planet, unlike the French, who are too busy not giving a damn. But there are definite redeeming aspects to their I-don't-give-a-damnism, the seeds of *jolie laide* being one of them.

ON *JOLIE LAIDE*, OR "UGLY PRETTY"

Strangeness is a necessary ingredient in beauty.

—BAUDELAIRE

Let's leave the obviously pretty women to men with no imagination.

—PROUST

French vocabulary lesson 101: *Jolie laide* is a French expression that directly translates into the awkward-sounding "ugly pretty," and it contains a world of nuance. *Jolie laide* is about beauty that does not conform to the standard norm. A woman who is *jolie laide* is beautiful in an unconventional way; her allure and perfection lie not only in the appeal of her imperfections and the way they defy the standard rubric of prettiness, but also in the persistent presence of an inner life that informs her outer appearance.

Perceptions of what makes a woman *jolie laide* are subjective, though in America Anjelica Huston is often bandied about as *jolie laide*, no doubt because her regal asymmetry defies the norms of magazine "pretty." There's the darkly idiosyncratic face of Sofia Coppola, and the mournful appeal of

Maggie Gyllenhaal. (When Gyllenhaal was told by Hollywood Overlords that she wasn't beautiful or sexy enough to make it on film, she replied: "You must have a boring idea of what being beautiful and sexy is.")

Naturally, France itself bursts with *jolie laide* women. There are classics like Anouk Aimée, Jeanne Moreau, or Simone Signoret; there's Coco Chanel and Edith Piaf. More contemporarily there's the disheveled loveliness of Élodie Bouchez (think French Björk), or Béatrice Dalle (that mouth! those eyes!) and countless others more ordinary but no less captivating.

Curiously, the term "jolie laide" has been appropriated by Anglophones, but if you ask your average French person what it means, you'll get a Gallic shrug. The term, which probably has its origins in the Serge Gainsbourg song "Laide jolie laide" (Ugly Pretty Ugly), is no longer part of the French vernacular—the concept, however, still burns brightly in the wide net they cast around this thing called "beauty." Appropriately enough, it could very well be Serge Gainsbourg's daughter, Charlotte Gainsbourg, who best embodies "jolie laideness." With her melancholic air and the vaguely awkward way she inhabits her lanky body, Gainsbourg has settled more luxuriously into her own persona with age, the very quirks we Anglos might "fix" taking on a certain cachet. I'm reminded of French actress Audrey Tautou, who once told *Allure* magazine: "I think when you're an adult, you start to like the very things that make you different. If you obsess about some defect, you make it obvious to everyone, and suddenly everyone is staring at just that defect. It's always like that. The more you hide something, the more it shows. But when you accept your defect, suddenly no one on earth sees it anymore. In fact, it becomes an asset."

An "asset"? What an interesting new way of making capital adjustments.

If an infinite gamut of romance or emotions exists for French women, an equally infinite gamut of possibilities for beauty exists outside the conventions of standard beauty. Like everyone else, French women adore their women's magazines, but they don't read them as gospel. They understand, to quote French singer Camille (*jolie laide* herself), that "if you stick to the beauty criteria of society and magazines, beauty becomes as much a handicap as ugliness. I'm convinced that we're all beautiful and ugly simultaneously." It's fair to say that most French women would agree. They understand that the true menace of the beauty jihad in women's magazines is the threat of being generically pretty and tragically the same.

French women, *jolie laide* or even just plain *laide*,

all seem genetically encoded with that uniquely French ability to play up their assets—which they do expertly, rather than anxiously try to sublimate them or transform them into the latest trademark look— and men sniff this sensual iconoclasm like so many free-floating pheromones. Ted Stanger, a former *Newsweek* journalist, author, and longtime American expatriate in France, summed up the male perspective in his book *Sacré-Français!*: "Pretty French women don't have a monopoly on sex appeal [in France]," he writes. "The game is open to all women. That's the first observation that any Anglo male will make when he's just landed on French soil. Max, one of my lawyer friends from Chicago, commented on this as soon as he arrived: 'Here in France, even unattractive women have something.' That might explain why you don't detect that antimale aggressiveness that you often encounter in America. In America you have to be 'beautiful and blonde' to seduce a man and have fun. So everyone—brunettes, redheads, those who are pretty a little, a lot, or not at all, obviously resent men."

If French women have a certain allure, it's because they grow up in a world where cookie-cutter beauty is not exalted—a world where it's generally okay not to give a damn about being anyone other than yourself, and where nuances, gray zones, and contradictions can coexist. Contradictions like beautiful and ugly. Like *jolie* and *laide*. That they live in a culture with such a flamboyantly generous concept is a wonderful thing. That they themselves have an appreciation for the concept—that they generally reject notions of packaged beauty and packaged lives—gives them enough feminine guile and freedom to assert themselves as sensual beings whether they're classically pretty, *jolie laide*, or just Plain Jane. And that, in a word, is truly sexy.

WHEN SMART IS SEXY

"If you want your man to stay in bed with you the next morning," my friend Marie once said, "you have to have something more to offer than just sex." In other words, you have to have a brain.

If the French enjoy sensual pleasures with unapologetic abandon, they're equally compelled by intellectual ones; the cerebral and the carnal have always gone together. Intelligence, wit, a sense of irony and insolence, the ability to spar and cultivate opinions (remember: in France being opinionated is a compliment)—these are but a few of the qualities that often trump classic coquetry. Be prepared to use your mind, then, when wading into amorous waters with the French. The aesthetics of intelligence count in France. (Think Eric Rohmer again, who dedicated an entire oeuvre to the eroticism of good conversation.) Gray matter and the lure of language are undeniably wrapped up in the seductive code; beauty and brains are entwined like so many limbs in dishy, rumpled bed linens.

The French esteem for that mélange of beauty and brains goes back ages, of course. Take Madame de Châtelet, who author David Bodanis once described as "Geena Davis, Mensa member, and one-time action film star, trapped in the eighteenth century." De Châtelet was alarmingly brilliant and even inspired Einstein centuries down the road, but as her cousin pointed out in a letter, she was also "a colossus in her limbs—a marvel of strength and a prodigy of clumsiness. She had terrible feet and formidable limbs." Not a problem, however, for France's favorite philosopher. "She was all passion and wits," Voltaire said, on why Madame de Châtelet burned a hole through his heart.

Madame de Staël was another fiercely intelligent *femme* to emerge in the eighteenth century. De Staël was a true radical who, despite her aristocratic pedigree, championed women's rights, religious tolerance, intellectual freedom, emancipation, and democracy at a time when the monarchy basically sucked. Her ideas so deeply challenged the reigning imperial zeitgeist of her times that Napoleon itched to be rid of her. "I shall break her, I shall crush her," he declared. "Let her keep quiet; it's the wisest counsel she can take." Madame de Staël, however, did not keep quiet.

But what tags along with de Staël over the centuries like a hound dog that will not go away is her reputation for defying the social conventions of traditional beauty. At a time when power dressing and the politics of appearance were at their apogee—a time when women were supposed to be graceful and ornamental—Madame de Staël was something of a buffoon, with an air of clownish dishevelment about her. She was ungainly, partial to wearing garish turbans and loud clothes, and she enjoyed receiving guests while wearing short petticoats and thin shirts (an eighteenth-century fashion faux pas). Even her breasts were a problem—they were positively mountainous, and de Staël wore low-cut dresses to show off their snowy peaks. (This so scandalized Napoleon that, as biographer J. Christopher Herold recounts, His Royal Smallness took one look at Her Royal Bigness and, aghast, remarked that she must have "fed" her own children—a low blow at a time when wet nurses were de rigueur.)

Madame de Staël, however, truly did not give a damn. She rejected the stiff corseted wedding-cake aesthetic of her time and refused to be simply decorative as a woman, and it served her well. Her wit, her charisma, her passion, and her crazy-brilliant mind kept powerful men flitting into her fire.

As de Staël's friend and colleague Isabelle de Charrière put it, women must imperatively "think from childhood about what you can obtain for yourself" to avoid the perils of becoming simply "a pretty goldfish circling endlessly in a Japanese fishbowl." Somehow this line of thinking has held strong over the centuries. French women may have an enduring reputation for being sexy, but being smart is invariably part of that package, which is why the beloved bimbo, enduring homecoming queen in America, does not have the same cachet in France.

The bimbo is a paragon of brainless beauty. In fact, it's the very happy surface sheen of her bimbosity—that preternatural glow unfettered by the furrowed brow of deep reflection—that makes her so sexy, because it implies an unthinking readiness to bounce into bed with her bodacious breasts and her big blond hair (bimbos love alliteration) with any come-hither strapping dude. There is something in the voluptuous pliancy of the bimbo, when you think about it, that conspires against Smart. Smart is prickly; it has edges, just like the smart woman, who is the bimbo's nemesis. The smart woman is generally seen as difficult, contentious, a bit of a menace, and filled with opinions that conspire against the Anglo bias for like-mindedness and consensus. In France, on the other hand, Smart has always been the New Sexy.

WHY ONE PLUS ONE
ALWAYS MAKES TWO

"Why does mad romantic love always appear French?" asks French journalist Guillemette Faure in her book *La France: Made in the USA.* "Undoubtedly because the passionate vision of love in France contradicts that of the average American, who willingly sees love as more of an extension of friendship." Faure learned this firsthand when, early in their relationship, her American boyfriend expressed his pleasure in their "great camaraderie." Faure was shocked. "I felt like I'd been stabbed in the heart. What a twit I was. I didn't realize that it was a compliment until I heard, during election campaigns, how American politicians presented their wives: 'She's my best friend.' "

Why should Faure be so astonished by this cultural discovery? For starters because French women don't necessarily expect their boyfriends or their spouses to be their best friends. They don't find the neutrality of best friendship, precluding as it does any whiff of sexuality, particularly redeeming, nor do they generally expect men to meet them halfway in the best-friends confidences and personal intimacies that are often shared among women. Embellishing this idea, French psychologist Danièle Flaumenbaum warns her readers that expecting your man to be your best friend is not only a way of asking him to relate to you like a woman; pushed to an extreme it's an unconscious way of asking him to relate to you like your *mother*. Not good. "Wanting to be understood without words and completely fulfilled by a man is asking him to understand and relate to us like a mother," writes Flaumenbaum. The desire for that kind of emotional "processing" quickly snuffs out the flames of passion and invariably leads to disappointment. "A part of us will always remain an unhappy, unsatisfied child."

Even more dicey consequences occur, by the way, if your man *is* actually able to understand you like your mother. According to Flaumenbaum, women end up loving their men "without wanting to make love to them. They love them but they don't want to be penetrated by them." Sounds a little like our friend Jenny who debuted earlier: overjoyed when her husband did all the housework—overjoyed when he was too tired to have sex as a result. Her husband was probably a great guy, too. In fact he was most likely her best friend.

Here, by the sheer force of their contrasting cultural values, French women throw back at us Siamese twins born of the same "confusion of love": one brings gender egalitarianism into marriage with a certain *Good Housekeeping* Vengeance; the other brings to marriage the precepts of our Tell-All confessional, girl-friendly culture that requires our mates to be an All-In-One package: lover, housecleaner, best friend, provider, partner, confidant, father, and . . . mother. These "invasive behaviors," Flaumenbaum advises, "block desire and make men retract like snails. Individuals can only desire one another when they are separate."

If we ratchet this up from the personal to the political—from the domestic living room to the Presidential Suite—it's easy to see why the French contradict our notion of what makes a good couple. As Faure suggests, the presidential couple is a model on a grandiose scale of what constitutes a good couple in the Anglo mind: not two separate individuals but One Couple, Indivisible, the First Lady being iconic here. She is a figurehead of rectitude and propriety; a cheerleader and a den mother, who always stands by her man. Together they are the ultimate best friends—in unison, in sync, in matching bathrobes. Even with her personal commitment to social crusades, the First Lady must sublimate a certain amount of personal independence or iconoclasm for the sake of at least impersonating a good political wife.

Veering from this norm rubs against the American grain in a big way. I can't help but recall Teresa Heinz, Senator John Kerry's wife, during Kerry's bid for the presidential nomination. Heinz fell right into this gray zone. She was independent, quirky, sophisticated, iconoclastic, and so unapologetically sensual that the American media didn't know what to make of her. As one reporter sniffed, "She's too European."

So it is with Ségolène Royal, France's first woman presidential contender—an unmarried (but long-term cohabitor) mother of four children, who took on the elitist macho French hegemony. Royal conspired against all things Anglo-Saxon. Her ability to navigate seamlessly the world of motherhood with the demands of the political arena and the eternal need to find just the right lipstick was something

French women all over the country could relate to, but it was her sex appeal and her unconventional relationship with her mate that got the outside world so hot and bothered. Her mélange of femininity and political power were so far off the American radar that Salon.com suggested she lives "in a parallel universe." And Andrew Hussey nearly gushed in *The Guardian*: "Royal's power is sexual. . . . She is flirtatious, stylish, and feminine in equal measures. . . . Is she Marie Antoinette or Marianne?"

The answer: like many of her French sisters, she's a little bit of both.

When it came to her relationship with her long-time companion François Hollande, Royal frequently called herself a "free woman." When her relationship with Hollande did indeed show signs of strain (when they were clearly not best friends), the French press did its share of grazing on the detritus, but the couple's personal issues were not perceived as a fatal flaw or a point of great public import. When asked whether they were a couple, Mr. Hollande simply replied: "It is not for us to either confirm or deny. Our lives belong to us.' " Everyone in France seemed to agree.

Similarly, when Sarkozy's then-wife told the press, "I don't see myself as a First Lady. That bores me. I am not politically correct," no one batted an eye. Echoes here of Anne-Aymone Giscard d'Estaing, who, when asked what she wanted to do as France's First Lady, replied, "To no longer be one." A similar response by a potential American First Lady could very well ruin her husband's career. But as Sarkozy once told *Le Figaro Magazine*, "In France you elect a candidate, not a family." True. And just as the presidential couple has carte blanche to stray from the mold of seamless unanimity, so, too, does the ordinary French couple.

Five

NATURE

On human nature and Mother Nature, the problem with eternal self-transformation, how looking sexy and feeling sexy are not the same thing, the difference between age-defying and age-denying, and what we have in common with birds and earthworms

The senses are the organs by which man communicates with the world outside himself.

—JEAN ANTHELME BRILLAT-SAVARIN

You're in a café in Paris, sitting next to a French woman. If there's any exasperating ooh-la-la stereotype of the French woman, here she is: Legs out to here. Infuriating lack of body fat. An alarming air of insouciance. The whole French package. One sultry look and legions would follow her to battle. Without fanfare she raises her arm to hail a waiter and—*wait*. What was that you just saw? Was that a little bush under her arm or have you been drinking too much cognac?

Upon closer inspection—well, you don't get actually to inspect closer but you do retreat behind your sunglasses so that you may stare unself-consciously at her rebellious armpit—and, yes, there they are: little tufts of fluffy under-brush contradicting everything you know about beauty norms and femininity; flipping its middle finger at personal hygiene; transgressing every rule about sexiness; boldly suggesting that this woman is part Madonna and part animal—and proud of it. This might be au naturel but it's just a tad too much *naturel* for you. In fact, it's a crime that should

----

be punishable with ten days of full-body waxing in a state penitentiary. All of which makes you wonder: What *is* it about French women and their armpit hair? And the answer is: more than you think.

OF COURSE MOST FRENCH women aren't walking around, looking like Borat. That said, I've often heard Americans comment, surreptitiously and in a state of mild shock, about beautiful French women in this semi-*sauvage* state. It's one of those throwaways about the French, like soap—as in, why don't they use it as often as us? I'm reminded of the first time an American friend visited our local Parisian *fromagère* and watched in stunned silence as the woman behind the counter sliced into a large round of Brie and handled the whole smelly wedge with her bare hands. "What?" my friend whispered. "No gloves?" This is the same friend who was astonished to find that we had an actual cheese cage in our kitchen.

Frankly, I was a bit astonished myself to find out that such things even exist. A cheese cage, for those of you unfamiliar with this charming French contraption, is exactly what it suggests: a small cage generally made of wood with steel mesh, in which various types of cheese can sit and ripen in peace. These cages are never put in the refrigerator because, like babies or wild orchids, cheese flourishes best at just the right room temperature. You may put your cheese cage on the ledge of your balcony at night for just the right natural chill (I did this for years until I accidentally knocked it off the ledge of our fourth-floor window and watched, horrified, as everything plummeted in a chaotic cheese free fall onto the ledge of the ground-floor apartment below), but refrigeration would permeate the plump little maturing cheeses with the acrid stench of refrigeration chemicals. Better to let the cheese coexist with the natural elements, which explains why our Parisian kitchen often has the malodorous fart smell of ripening Camembert. This bouquet, shall we say, is perfectly acceptable to the French—far more acceptable than the no-smell of an overly sanitized kitchen. Kitchens, like humans, are supposed to breathe with life.

"Why is this cheese in jail?" my friend asked the first time she saw my caged *fromage*. Okay, so we've come a long way from the woman who debuted our chapter. Let's come full circle: when it comes to the realm of the senses, the French have a way of accepting and even embracing the unruly luxuriance of nature; they even, more notably, have a way of accepting the vagaries of age with more inspired realism. The metaphor of food here is both cliché and perfectly fitting. Anne-Marie, who's been teaching French to students in Los Angeles for more than twenty years, offers this observation: "My American students are very detached from the real world and very squeamish. They are so used to the fake or the processed that when they see the real thing, they don't get it. Or when they see the fake, they think it's the real thing. When I teach them the origin of the word 'ham' in French—*jambon*—for example, I tell them that it means leg. When you eat ham, you are eating the leg of the pig. 'Oh, gross! Don't gross us out!' is what the kids always scream. And I ask them, 'Do you think that pigs grow in slices? Where do you think ham comes from?' These kids are grossed out by almost anything that is not hygienically sealed up. There is a disconnect from nature, and that becomes a disconnect from the senses, from the sensual world overall."

Without overstating things, it's fair to say that the French are all *about* that connection to nature. And that connection informs not just what the French woman eats; it informs sex, sex appeal, and seduction itself. Think Brigitte Bardot, that paragon of feral French sensuality. For the French, true sexiness generally has a touch of the wild in it, which is why I've always admired a curious but rightful passage written by Edith Kunz in her book *Fatale*. "Although spectacular hairdos can be seen at gala balls in France, the [French] ladies also know how to let their hair down. They are aware that having a hairdo sprayed in place can throw out a cautionary barrier to men, who are intimidated about approaching such an organized creature."

Though Kunz dates herself with the reference to "sprayed hairdos" (we forgive her), she certainly hits an interesting nerve with the idea that for many French women, letting your hair down has more sexy currency than projecting an image of calculated perfection. Kunz calls this state of French grace the illusive charms of "seductive disarray" and "accidental allure"—two terms infused with the happy coexistence of contradictions and the tousled bed-headed idea that trying too hard to be "sexy" is somehow unsexy. What would happen if we all stopped trying so hard?

What would happen, in other words, if as Véronique Vienne once asked, "sex pundits stopped advising us to rekindle our connubial pleasures with scented candles, massage oils, and red satin teddies, and instead extolled the virtues of the chaotic, the disheveled, the hasty intercourse?" *What, indeed?* "Domesticity would be fraught with fewer dangers if partners didn't have to measure up to unrealistic standards of romance."

There are, of course, countless dangers of domesticity that lead to unrealistic standards of romance, not the least of which is domesticity itself, uniquely designed as it seems to squeeze the juice out of those "connubial pleasures." I'm reminded of a *New York Times* article by Maureen Dowd titled "Men Just Want Mommy," in which she singles out a scene in the film *Spanglish*: an American chef (Adam Sandler) is married to an "overachieving, overexercized, unfaithful she-monster." Overjoyed to learn of her husband's promotion, she jumps on him and humps away like a praying mantis in increasingly fitful waves of orgasmic frenzy. As she reaches a strained but very efficient climax, phlegmatic hubby looks up at her and asks: "You don't even need me for this, do you?"

- - - - - - - - -

To which she replies, well, er, no. Sandler—can we blame the poor guy?—later falls in love with their hot Latin nanny. She is, needless to say, oozing with sensual disarray and accidental allure.

Dowd cites this scene as evidence of a trend—men hooking up with women whose job it is to care for them in some way: secretaries, nannies, etc. "So, was the feminist movement some sort of cruel hoax?" she asks. "The more women achieve, the less desirable they are?" But maybe, in all due respect to Dowd, it's not as wickedly antifeminist as that. Maybe men don't want mommy. Maybe they just want a little reprieve from all that "overachieving" and "overexercising." Maybe men *and* women need a little reprieve from it.

Reprieve, however, is not an operative word in today's culture of self-improvement and self-transformation, and nowhere is this more apparent than in the glare that surrounds women "of a certain age" in America. (That would be forty-plus, for even if forty is the new thirty, it is still, let's be real, nestled right there next to fifty.) While older French women are generally enjoying their lives of accrued sensual disarray and accidental allure, American women are often busy whipping themselves into shape with a vengeance or feeling like guilty slackers for not doing so. And that's because a blazing feel-good paradox sears its way through our culture, sealing in its own juices. Take a look at any magazine for women forty-plus: Celebrations of age come with a clarion call for an aesthetic that still emulates youth in all its age-defying firmness, with an accompanying Protestant work ethic that would make any good-hearted Quaker weep. *Fearless at Forty! Fabulous at Fifty! Scintillating at Sixty!* You can achieve this all—*the clothes! the makeup! the confidence!* (preferably with tight abs and a firm butt)—through "age-defying body secrets" that will help you to "think yourself younger."

To achieve those "ageless looks" and that "gravity-proof" body, we're deluged with techniques and workouts and even hourly breakdowns, like this one brought to you by *More* magazine designed to literally keep you on your toes: Start your day at 6:00 A.M. with an unforgiving rise out of your bed's cozy warmth ("Stop pressing 'snooze'") and get cracking! From morning to night on an hourly basis you should "pump iron at your desk," "eat to energize," "do a face check," "muscle up your memory," "do number-based tasks," "go decaf," "prep for an afternoon snack," "break a sweat," "do Kegels" and "dish up for dinner. By 8:00 P.M., you may "have sex," but only after you "take your calcium supplement" and before you "exercise your intellect" and "rejuvenate your face." (Anyone exhausted yet?) As the hours tick by, so do the decades. Here's your 50-year personal style grid: Go for "granny skirts at 20, curvy and corseted at 30, perfecting your legs at 40, rethinking wrinkles at 50, better sex at 60, skinny jeans at 70, pirate sleeves at 80, pearls and Levi's at 90."

But the real pot of gold at the end of this hectic rainbow (provided you continue to *tune up! tone up! pump up!*) is this: You can finally "Be Yourself." You finally "Know Who You

Are," since, let's face it, until now life has been one long putting aside of your authentic self in search of being someone or something else. By the time you've mastered all this ageless perfection, you might actually be well into your Golden Years, but it doesn't matter because you'll finally have a sense of self and you'll look Absolutely Fabulous.

What's wrong with this picture? Is it any surprise that, as we take primers from, say, *Vogue*'s top models (*Twenty years later, they're back, hotter than ever, and telling all about aging!*), so many women aren't feeling that hot? Take a good whiff of the graying *air du temps* and it seems like we're all obsessed with sex yet feeling strangely unsexy. Something seems to be missing in all this strenuous, joyless pining away to be sexy. Are we actually age-defying or age-denying? Growing up and being a grown-up in America has never seemed like so much work, nor has it ever seemed so curiously childlike.

Meanwhile, here's the clincher: older French women are doing quite well, *merci beaucoup*. In fact, while the amount of sex they have is not the point, it's hard to sweep this salient detail under the carpet: according to an exhaustive comparative Franco-American sex study conducted by Alain Giami, French women of fifty-plus apparently have more active sex lives than we do—*without* all the static. Why?

Let's start with this: huffing and puffing on the treadmill of personal transformation is no picnic, and French women know it. They're generally suspicious of the American-style culture of constant self-transformation, which draws you into its undertow with the promise of a Totally New, Improved, Much Better You while its evil twin suggests that There Is Something Very Wrong With You. French women sense strains of joyless utilitarianism here that conspire not only against all that bon vivantism but that smack of a certain puritan self-denial gone awry. No wonder French women aren't overly concerned with trying to break a sweat in the gym every morning or pump iron at their desks or eat to energize or do Kegels before dinner. In fact, they look like they *do* press the snooze button and forget to do their numbers-based tasks and maybe have a little "chaotic and disheveled intercourse" along the way.

Older French women also tend to approach menopause, that Tollbooth on the Superhighway of Life, with less static accompanying them down the tarmac. In America, on the other hand, it's become something of a demarcation zone for ongoing debates that reveal deep age angst. With her book *Sex and the Seasoned Woman*, Gail Sheehy joins the ranks of others who exalt the passage to those Golden Years (with a little help from sex toys and "soul connection" sex-therapy spa retreats), though other equally seasoned women aren't so convinced how golden these years are. "What's So Hot About 50?" Daphne Merkin inquired in an essay about Sheehy's book that says everything we need to know in its title: "Sex and the female boomer is *not* booming." Erica Jong added her observation that all this age angst "would not be surprising in

Italy or France or Europe. There are Italian sexpot actresses who are much older. But somehow in our strangely puritanical yet sex-obsessed country, people are shocked. That's uniquely American." But it's perhaps author Toni Bentley who hit the nail on the head when, in reviewing Sheehy's book, she suggests that the real issue that remains to be tackled—the real subject "which merits far more depth and attention than even the best vibrator can provide"—is aging. And what about, Bentley asks, this thing that should go along with it, "this intangible component called dignity? How to have it, how to keep it, how to teach it?"

What *about* all that?

If being more at peace with human nature and with Mother Nature is a start, then French women "of a certain age" surely have a leg up in the dignity department. Of course, they do their share of age-defying like everyone else; vanity is universal. Yet there remains in France the enduring bias that women are beautiful when they've accrued a certain knowingness, and that this knowingness comes from age and experience. Most French women aren't overly concerned about pining away to stay young because many of them are too busy enjoying being grown-ups. Of course, it certainly helps that France is a grown-up culture, not a youth culture, where forty- and fifty-year-olds get to have all the fun. French grown-ups are still active participants in that "erotic in daily life," with all its seductions and pleasures, and they tend to enjoy whatever sensual license and daily pleasures

come their way without fretting about staying forever twei
in the process. This brings sharp and sobering new light to
what Edith Wharton once wrote: "The French woman is in
nearly all respects as different as possible from the average
American woman. The French woman is more grown-up.
Compared with the women of France the average American
woman is still in kindergarten."

Kindergarten? That's quite a jab. But let's be honest: Wharton *was* onto something, wasn't she? Don't French grown-ups
seem like . . . grown-ups?

One hint about the nature of this state of grace comes
our way from French writer/academician Isabelle de Courtivron. A professor at MIT and author of several books, de
Courtivron looks at age through the prism of her own experience as a French woman living in America in an essay titled
"Midlife Memoirs and the Bicultural Dilemma." And in de
Courtivron's eyes, it's Colette, seeped as she is in the culture
of seduction, who shines brightly as an archetype. As Colette
wrote in *Break of Day*, there comes an age for every woman
"when the only thing that is left for her is to enrich her own
self." De Courtivron describes this approach to age as the
"Colettian dilemma," or more precisely a mind-set that asks
of women to be "acutely aware of the approaching if unjust
social destiny [and] to squeeze pleasure until the last drop; to
remain lucid about this unavoidable situation and attentive
to its compensations; to love and understand men enough not
to begrudge their own limiting realities; to build plenitude

so that when the moment to step back has arrived, it brings with it the challenge of elegantly negotiating this turn rather than bitterly decrying it, or shrilly proclaiming it."

Sounds like a great way to approach that "intangible component called dignity" to me.

Colette, with her flamboyant hair, her creative "plenitude" and her polymorphous sex life, was all about seductive disarray and accidental allure. She also lived with that keen sense of the "brevity of time" and "the immediacy of pleasure," which, as French women generally understand, does not revolve around attaining a state of ageless perfection in gravity-defying leaps of cosmetic reinvention and unforgiving daily regimes, nor taking cues from a burlesque (or can we call it "undignified"?) style autocracy that asks women to wear "skinny jeans at seventy" or "pirate sleeves at eighty." Nor is it about happily withdrawing to a manless tundra where desire—even the pain of its diminished signal bleeping out in the dark of night—is denied. They also know, while we're at it, that it's not about trying to achieve Mind-Blowing Sex or Thirty-Second Orgasms in our seventies or eighties while we wonder where all the vim and vigor has gone.

If French women aren't preoccupied with being *Fabulous at Forty!* or *Fantastic at Fifty!*, it is not to say that they move away from their feminine centers as they age. On the contrary, they continue to enjoy that culture of seduction with its vanities, while remaining "lucid" about the inevitability of age. In France there is less concern about "fixing" Mother

Nature or human nature, because you don't "fix" yourself in France—you cultivate yourself. You don't fuss over the "right" way to do something; you work with who you are and create your own personal narrative, and, in accepting that the brevity of time is inevitable, you fill your life with as much pleasure as possible.

This is what makes the difference, to quote de Courtivron, between the "mature mistresses" we see in France and the "midlife militants" we have in America, where the flip side of the Fabulous-at-Forty-and-Fifty, Age-Defying-Alpha Sisterhood is a certain hardened resignation. After all, why bother getting back on a new treadmill at forty or fifty or sixty when you've spent your whole life feeling enslaved by the treadmill? And who needs men, anyhow? Isn't it time you finally took a break and let yourself go?

Julie Barlow, coauthor of *Sixty Million Frenchmen Can't Be Wrong* and *The Story of French*, once described a hiking trip she took with her girlfriends; at one point Barlow and her girlfriends were joined by an American woman hiker in her late fifties. "She was heavyset and she had clearly let herself go physically," said Barlow. "She laughed when she saw men hitting on us and said, 'Thank God, I'm done with all that.' This was typically American. You'd rarely hear a French woman say that. You'd rarely hear a French woman so easily dismiss the loss of her feminine appeal."

There's great truth in Barlow's words. French women continue to cultivate themselves as women and feminine creatures, even as they tend to reject the unforgiving messages and regimes that feed on women's insecurities about age and provoke such labored extremes. With trademark realism, they view age as an inescapable part of nature's grand plan—a personal destiny to which we're all tethered. No one emphasized this to French women with more passion and eloquence than Simone de Beauvoir. To read her chapter on aging in *The Second Sex* is to experience realism with excruciating candor. "Old age is life's parody," she wrote, "whereas death transforms life into a destiny: in a way it preserves it by giving it the absolute diversion. Death does away with time."

De Beauvoir rakes us over the age-defying coals in describing nearly every form of emotional, social, and biological tribulation associated with growing older; and while some of her darker observations are (happily) outdated, she gives voice to the realism and knowingness that seems hard-wired in French women. As they age, women not only "begin at last to view the world through their own eyes," writes de Beauvoir; the older woman also reaches a place where, having lived long enough in the presence of men, she understands men "as no man does, for she has seen in man not the image on public view but the contingent individual, the creature of circumstance, that each man in the absence of his peer shows himself to be. She knows women also, for they show themselves without reserve only to other women: she has been behind the scenes."

All of which explains why you'll probably never see a

French woman with a T-shirt that reads "Life Begins at Seventy." Because it doesn't.

PLATITUDES ABOUT SEXY older French women may abound; still, it is true that these creatures do not lament the injustice of age, fight against it, or dramatize its pros or the cons with quite the same vengeance as their Anglo sisters. Nor do they express the same subtle sense of outrage, as Daphne Merkin once described in a *New York Times* article, that older men avoid older women "because they sense the impending shadow of nongenerativity like a negative pheromone."

French men bait their hooks for younger women like men the world over; still, why don't we hear this discontent so vigorously expressed by French women? Is it possible that French men appreciate older French women more than their American counterparts? I asked Alain Giami the questions point-blank, to which he replied: "We can look at those questions in two ways. We could say that French men are attracted to older women and to women of their same age. But we could also ask the question: Do American women remove themselves from the sexual market because they're not interested in sex anymore? They may continue to be sexy, with cosmetic surgery and so forth, but to look sexy is not enough to sustain a sexual relationship. So perhaps they don't want to have as much sex."

That's quite a zinger.

- - - - - - - - -

Giami then added the somewhat distressing hypothesis that if the granddaughters of Colette seem to leverage better than us in the love/sex department, it's perhaps because they know something about enduring relationships with men. "The possibility of having sex after fifty," he said, "is strongly dependent on the capacity to be in a relationship."

Speaking with Giami made me think about Freud, and wonder whether what French women know about love and sex might have something to do with what they know about Freud. In America, Freud has been dethroned by a huge number of à la carte therapies. In France, however, Freud is part of a Holy Trinity of Psychoanalysis: First there was Freud. Then there was Lacan. Then there was Foucault.

As my friend Ann put it, "If anyone tells you that they completely understand Foucault and Lacan, they are lying." We'll leave it at that. As for Freud, he invented the concept of the libido, after all, and the notion that sexual repression creates sexual obsession. (Oppress it—obsess over it.) "Analyze any human emotion," he wrote, "no matter how far it may be removed from the sphere of sex, and you are sure to discover somewhere the primal impulse, to which life owes its perpetuation." In other words, everything boils down to sex. Try finding a cultural gatekeeper in France who would disagree with that.

Now, this is a vast simplification, but there was a time when Freud was equally hot in America. All of our personal issues could be "fixed" with the right program, including our sexual issues, which were our mother's fault or our father's fault and which festered in the dark cellar of our unconscious like large portobello mushrooms. Freud offered a system that could make love work—even though Freudian analysis took so long you might be dead by the time it actually kicked in. That said, while the "fix it" function remains on overdrive in America, the Freudian idea that we might be driven by primal instincts we can't control has been largely swept under the rug in America. This is partly because these primal instincts imply that we're all part of the great Animal Kingdom and not necessarily part of the great Kingdom of God. If we were to lift that rug, we'd find innumerable pieces of complicated sociohistorical and religious debris, for lack of a better word. We do not intend to do the housecleaning in these pages. But we can't ignore the fact that despite these hard-core times of ours, there endures the notion in America that the animal kingdom is dirty—morally dirty, just like sex. (For explanations, please see the Kingdom of God.) For equally complicated reasons that can't fit snugly in these pages, let us simply say that the French have not been influenced by this type of thinking.

"In France we accept that we're part of the animal kingdom," says my friend Christophe, an established journalist who works on both sides of the Atlantic. "We share the same DNA as dogs, birds, earthworms. There are things that animals don't understand about the world. There are things that we human beings don't understand as well. We can't see ultraviolet. We can't hear ultrasound. For the French, there's a more humble acceptance of the instinctual part of our nature, the animal side. The French go more with their instincts. If someone is fat or thin, rich or poor . . . what matters is how you feel about someone on a very instinctual level. You make love with more passion and you go with your passions. You don't try to control the basic stuff. You have no control over death, let alone emotions, attractions, passions. Live and let live. That is the French attitude—*ça m'a pris*."

Ça m'a pris. Which means: *It just took hold of me. I couldn't resist. Passion got the better of me.* I'm reminded of an older French woman quoted in a book by Elisabeth Weissman titled *Un âge nommé désir* (An Age Called Desire). "I want to live everything with the most density possible," she says. "My relationship to time is totally different. I am so conscious that life might escape me at any moment, that everything has become keener and more distilled. . . . I tell myself: All this happiness still, but for how long? So I devour life."

To devour life. Such is the "Colettian dilemma" expressed in its most distilled form. I'm reminded of what Lincoln once said: *It's not the years in your life that count but the life in your years.* Too bad we have to wait to be grown-ups to figure that one out.

THE SIXTH SENSE OF DESIRE

The discovery of a new dish does more for human happiness than the discovery of a star.

—JEAN ANTHELME BRILLAT-SAVARIN

Sharing food with another human being is an intimate act that should not be indulged in lightly.

—M. F. K. FISHER

It's a cliché to associate food with sex, and the French with both. And, of course, you don't have to be Freud to understand that human beings have a deep compensatory relationship to food. We might not have all the love and sex we want in our lives—in fact, we might be desperately lonely or miserably horny—but we can always find solace in a dark chocolate éclair, a sugar-glazed fruit tart, or, what the hell, a bag of chips. And that's because hunger and eating are often sublimated experiences of erotic, sensual, or emotional intensity missing in life.

With this in mind, it's not far-fetched to suggest that obesity in America is partly a manifestation of the extent to which our nation, in increasingly packaged times, has become sensuality-starved. Food has never been more glorified or more commodified in America, where a food-as-entertainment culture has given birth to the culture of food porn. Wikipedia, that Encyclopedia of All Things on Earth, describes the latter this way: "Much in the same way that pornography can be a vicarious substitute for actual sexual relations, 'food porn' is seen as a substitute for actually cooking and eating the food in question." Just as sex has become something of a bedroom sport, cooking in America—commodified and clattering with its celebrity chefs and extreme epicureans—has become a kitchen sport.

Now, much of this is delightfully absent from French culture. Yes, France is home to haute cuisine and a venerated coterie of renowned chefs whose culinary talents go back centuries, but the French are infinitely more relaxed about gastronomy and its pleasures. Maybe that's because they've been at it for so long, or because they have yet to discover the hazards of the Food Network, or because affluence hasn't spurred the kind of mass marketing of food elitism you have in America. Everyone in France, even the guy who fixes the busted tailpipe on your old Renault, is born with an inkling of how to do basic things with food that seem positively medieval: how to devein a goose liver, for example, or pluck a chicken, or make a simple roux. And while we're at it, nearly everyone in France will concede that what's behind the desire to cook and eat is a primal appetite driven by physical desire, an aspect of the human condition so fundamental that Jean Anthelme Brillat-Savarin qualified it as a bona fide sixth sense.

Born in the cultural megawattage of eighteenth-century France, Brillat-Savarin was a politician, lawyer, and musician, among other occupations, but he is best known as a great gastronome and author of *The Physiology of Taste: Or, Meditations on Transcendental Gastronomy.* In this lavish opus, as dense as cheesecake and just as delicious, Brillat-Savarin pays homage to this sixth sense of physical desire. It is this sense, he writes, "which draws the two sexes together so that they may procreate"; and it is also this sixth sense which, since time immemorial, "nurtures romantic love, coquetry, and fashion, and above all coquetry." (Brillat-Savarin is quick to emphasize coquetry, "which was born in France, which has no other name than its French one, and which the world's choicest souls come every day to study in Paris, their spiritual capital.")

In other words without this sixth sense—without physical desire driving the primal appetites that inspire us to eat, savor, and make love—we humans would not be here to wax poetic about, say, the best way to grill a flank steak or what exactly you're supposed to do with a endive that's spent three months in your refrigerator. "Everything subtle and ingenious" is due to this sixth sense, he writes, "to the desire, the hope, the gratitude that spring from sexual union.... Such is, then, in good truth, the genesis of even the most abstract sciences: they are nothing more than the immediate result of our continuous attempt to gratify the sense we have developed."

In other words everything boils down to physical desire, which eventually boils down to sex.

It is easy to forget momentarily that this great gastronome was writing about food; about partridge wings, turkey cock, stuffed pheasant (best eaten "within a week after its death"), snipe, venison, pike, oysters, and the aphrodisiac properties of the truffle. It is easy to overlook his advice about veal fillets larded with fat bacon, or enormous pâté de foie gras shaped like bastions, or wild quail and the fig pecker, which, if you're curious about this kinky-sounding forest creature, is best eaten this way: "Take the fine fat little bird, salt him lightly, pull out his gizzard, stuff him deftly into your mouth, bite him off sharply close to your fingertips, and chew with vigor: there will flow from him enough juice to fill your whole mouth, and you will enjoy a taste experience unknown to the common herd." The list goes on and on, along with the social, intestinal, and spiritual attributes of all things considered.

- - - - - - - - -

What's so enticing about Brillat-Savarin, beyond his scrumptiously baroque style and digressive anecdotes about herbivorous beasts and gluttonous Parisians, is the strangely contemporary aroma of his reflections. Shades of Mireille Guiliano's *French Women Don't Get Fat* waft off the hot plate when Brillat-Savarin reminds women that the pleasure of gourmandism is paramount; that in addition to its many social attributes, it "adds brilliancy to the eyes, freshness to the skin, and more firmness to all the muscles." It also does wonders for "the sagging of these muscles which causes wrinkles, beauty's fiercest enemy." Impoverished diet divas who suffer on the treadmills of abstinence end up "misers" afflicted with "the pallor of illness, the wasted scrawniness of poverty and the deep wrinkles of a feebled senility." Meanwhile, those women who are true sensualists and who "know how to eat are comparatively ten years younger than those to whom this science is a stranger."

Pass the partridge pie, *s'il vous plaît*.

As Guiliano herself noted, "French women seduce the way they order and savor food, with the sly complicity of stealing a taste from the other's plate or feeding our lover a particularly choice morsel. For the French, the sex appeal of eating is second nature." Brillat-Savarin would have agreed. In fact,

the sex appeal of eating might be second nature for
French women, but it doesn't stop there; nature itself
has sex appeal for them. French women, generally
speaking, still see themselves as *part* of nature, as
sentient creatures who, like the wild boar or the fat-
tened pigeon, are put on earth, as Brillat-Savarin
reminds us, "to be born, to move about, to eat, to
sleep, to procreate and to die." (*The Physiology of Taste*
is not without a detailed meditation on death, which
Brillat-Savarin qualifies as "the complete interrup-
tion of sensual relations.")

Remarkably, most French people still know
where their food comes from and how it grows (they
are maniacal gardeners; I have yet to meet a French
country-dweller who does not lovingly maintain a
vegetable garden of some sort) and why you can't—
and shouldn't—get a really great tomato in the winter. There is something inherently sexy in knowing
basic things about nature; it links one to the instinc-
tive and intuitive side of life in a way that bodes well
for love and sex. If French women remain more connected to the sixth sense of physical desire, more
attuned to its animal needs and nuances, it is partly
for this reason.

Food is sensuality writ edible, and cooking is
a supreme form of seduction; thus, as campy as it
sounds, French women will tell you that the best

way to a man's heart is still via his stomach. That said, you don't have to drain your gizzards over the perfectly crafted meal. Understanding the alchemy of basic elements and knowing how to make things from scratch has more long-term sensual import than one might imagine. It suggests an ability to seize the moment; to please and to pleasure easily. It implies the capacity to approach life with a certain improvised flair so that when love walks in the room, it can be fed. The romantic six-course meal with all the trimmings might be a sublimated experience of more erotic things to come, but a simple herb omelet simmered in butter and savored with a bottle of cold white wine can be just as seductive. In the same way that the simple pleasures of shared gourmandism can do more for conjugal woes than all the five-star restaurants and marriage therapy combined (as Brillat-Savarin also tells us).

On that note, I've always admired a French girl-friend who shall remain unnamed, and whose mar-riage, I believe, was held together largely by her ability to roll with the punches and cook with the same ease. All hell could be breaking loose and the cupboards bare, but she could still make a heavenly piecrust (one of baking's true tribulations) out of half a pack of graham crackers and some butter. "It is no problem," she would say. And so it wasn't. We're back to the notion that you can get more with less, that great sensual import can be had in small, seemingly ordinary things, and that the relationship between the erotic and the culinary are forever entwined. "I am just as interested in describing what a piece of chocolate tastes like as I am in evoking how a great orgasm feels," author Marie Darrieussecq once told *The Guardian*. (With that in mind, it's interesting to note that where we refer to a man's tight abdominals as his "six-pack," the French refer to them as his "chocolate tablets." Sounds a lot more tempting than beer.)

All this reminds me of a summer long ago when I was stuck in tremendous traffic, heading out of Paris en route to the south of France. As a dense herd of Northern European motorists converged onto the country's main diesel-choked, southbound highway, I began to fiddle with the radio for relief and stumbled on a conversation between two French gastronomes. The subject: the phenomenology of the green bean.

Now, this was no foodie tête-à-tête, laced with the kind of mildly fetishistic and slightly smug epicurean snobbism that, personally, has always given me a craving for a Big Mac. No. These two individuals—a man and a woman, of course—spoke at great length about the inherent sexiness of the green bean: how it grows (with the sun bathing its nascent roots, soil moist, warm, and fertile), ways to prepare it (snap off both ends, please; don't forget to remove that infinitesimal and irrelevant string), and so on. And then there was intellectual and historical arcana that went on for hours, which regrettably I've all but forgotten but which made the bean—the slim, unassuming, heretofore unsexy green bean—a mighty metaphor for how the entire natural universe can reside in something the size of a pencil. You've got to love the French for this alone. They get heavy about politics and philosophy, but they get equally heavy about green beans.

As I listened, rapt (I was halfway to the Mediterranean in no time), I realized that I would never again look at the green bean in quite the same light. I suddenly got very hungry and wanted, badly, to arrive at my destination and cook a few beans. I had an insatiable appetite, quite unexpectedly, to feed and be fed.*

- - - - - - - - - - - - - - - - - -

*Long before Atkins and other diet gurus came on the scene, Brillat-Savarin was espousing sound diet theories in a humorous meditation on obesity. After more than 500 conversations with flamboyant French fatties (all of them lovers of macaroons, meringues, and melted grease), he concluded that along with pacing yourself as you eat, "the principal [sic] cause of any fatty corpulence is always a diet overloaded with starchy and farinaceous elements." In other words, enjoy yourself, eat in moderation, and hold the carbs.

Six

ART DE VIVRE

On the difference between making a living and having a life, breaking the codes of the bourgeoisie, sex after kids, and the reason why your life won't end up going to hell in a handbasket if you let your proverbial hair down

I don't feel guilt. Whatever I wish to do, I do.

—JEANNE MOREAU

H ere's another American joke that you probably won't hear in France:

On a chain of beautiful deserted islands in the middle of nowhere, the following people are stranded:

Two Italian men and one Italian woman

Two French men and one French woman

Two German men and one German woman

Two Greek men and one Greek woman

Two British men and one British woman

Two Japanese men and one Japanese woman

Two Chinese men and one Chinese woman

Two Irish men and one Irish woman

Two American men and one American woman

One month later, on these absolutely stunning deserted islands in the middle of nowhere, the following things have occurred:

- - - - - - - - - -

One Italian man has killed the other Italian man for the Italian woman.

The two French men and the French woman are living happily together in a ménage à trois.

The two German men have a strict weekly schedule of alternating visits with the German woman.

The two Greek men are sleeping together and the Greek woman is cooking and cleaning for them.

The two British men are waiting for someone to introduce them to the British woman.

The two Japanese men have faxed Tokyo and are awaiting instructions.

The two Chinese men have set up a pharmacy, a liquor store, restaurant, and laundry, and have gotten the woman pregnant in order to supply employees for their stores.

The two Irish men have divided the island into north and south and set up a distillery. They do not remember if sex is in the picture because it gets somewhat foggy after a few liters of coconut whiskey. However, they're satisfied because the British aren't having any fun.

The two American men are contemplating suicide, because the American woman will not shut up and complains relentlessly about her body, the true nature of feminism, what the sun is doing to her skin, how she can do anything they can do, the necessity of fulfillment, the equal division of household chores, how sand and palm trees make her look fat, how her last boyfriend respected her opinion and treated her more nicely than they do, and how her relationship with her mother is the root cause of all her problems, and why didn't they bring a damn cell phone so they could call 911 and get them all rescued off the godforsaken deserted island in the middle of freaking nowhere so she can get her nails done and go shopping.

Okay, so it's a stereotype *and* it's politically incorrect. Still, why is the French woman always depicted as a languorous bon vivant while the American woman is portrayed as someone who's sexy as a doorstop? Why does the French woman always seem ready to embrace the virtues (if not literally, then surely metaphorically) of "chaotic, disheveled intercourse" while the American woman is too concerned about breaking a fingernail? Why, on a similar note, does everyone want go to Paris when they fall in love?

Don't answer. We know. We go to Paris to off-load our cultural baggage and momentarily stop worrying about the true nature of feminism and our body fat and what the sun is doing to our skin and the equal division of household chores and what we think of our parents and ex-boyfriends and all the rest. We go to Paris to upload a new sensory experience, one that in its radiant and unfettered sensuality knocks us off our feet. "Holy shit! Who made all this?" Carmela asked in *The Sopranos* when she took her first look at Paris. Then she got a little weepy, and added: "Makes you look at yourself differently."

- - - - - - - - - -

And so it does. No wonder millions of us go to France every year. What a relief to step out of ourselves and slip into something a little more . . . comfortable. Because after years of marriage, kids, and work, many of us are like the multi-armed Indian goddess Kali without the sex drive. Kali, you'll be reminded, is the divine Mother Goddess and slightly malevolent feminine force who is often depicted topless, with baubles, bangles, and the biggest breasts this side of Bombay. She usually has one foot on her thigh and the other on her husband. Hmm . . .

Meanwhile, even after they've entered the Kingdom of Coupledom and its Fiefdom of Babyhood, French women still seem to keep their libidos intact, or at least look like they still care. Many of us have marveled at these creatures in Paris: How they manage to push strollers and walk in high heels on cobblestones the size of grapefruits without twisting an ankle is one small miracle. How they don't seem battered by their jobs, their kids, their husbands, or their desire to look like the decorous dolls in *Desperate Housewives* is another small miracle. It can't be as easy as slipping into a pair of La Perla panties, so what's the trick?

Art de vivre is one of those cute French clichés that have been walking around with a beret and a baguette forever, but there's more to this celebrated term than you might imagine. In short it's hard to want to *have* sex, let alone feel sexy, when you lead an unsexy life (harder still to hop in bed after an exhausting day and act like a Victoria's Secret model when

you feel like Kirstie Alley in *Fat Actress*). And true *art de vi*
sexy, but perhaps not exactly in the way we think it is, because
it conspires against many of the cultural beliefs that turn us
into those raging multiarmed deities in the first place.

For French author Véronique Vienne these cultural beliefs
are woven into *Seven Deadly Virtues*. Self-improvement ranks
high on the list here; other deadly virtues include "constantly
raising the bar, having what it takes, wasting no time, being organized, being goal-oriented," and "being righteous." In other
words, flipped on its head or taken to an extreme, almost every
virtue to which we Americans are beholden quickly becomes a
vice to the French eye. Maybe we all need to get a little more existential about life. Or as my friend Jean-Michel puts it: "American women need to fuck up a little more. Be late for something.
Let the homework be late occasionally. Let the kids miss a play-
date. Drink a little too much with their husbands from time to
time. I'm not talking about crashing a car and getting a DUI.
I'm talking about letting go a little bit; letting up."

This is certainly one way of suggesting that whether you're
stranded on that beautiful island with no sunscreen, no cell
phone, and no manicure—or whether you're just going about
your business, trying to do your daily life with its wolfish
appetite for tormenting tasks, lists, and vexing obligations—
there are simple, sensual pleasures to be had in daily life if
we'd only let our proverbial hair down (and stop worrying
about how it looks when we do).

These simple pleasures are all entwined in *art de vivre*.

- - - - - - - - -

Let us put an emphasis on the word *simple*. You can't buy *art de vivre*. You don't need a big house or a turbo stainless-steel infrared barbecue for *art de vivre*. Sheer stuff, no matter how utterly excellent it might be, is still just stuff. The holy trinity of essentials—a simple bottle of wine, bread, and good company—is all that's needed for a deeply satisfying moment, and the French have an almost promiscuous capacity to create those moments. Leisure is practically a national preoccupation, relatively speaking at least. The French thirty-five-hour workweek might seem baroque to those who'd work thirty-five hours *a day* if they could, but the notion that everyone has the right to repose is so ingrained in the French consciousness that even inconveniences that would be crimes against the state in America—the two-hour lunch that shuts down the boutique where you're planning on shopping during *your* own lunch break; the Saturday supermarket pileups that happen because everything's closed on Sunday—are accepted with a shrug. Taking the time to step *off* the treadmill is as important, if not more so, as being on it. Thus, the French woman will also organize her life around the imperatives of *not* doing things—a concept so antithetical to the American way that I get exhausted just thinking about it.

The French are professional sensualists ("a job," author Joel Achenbach once writes, "that doesn't exist in America outside certain zip codes in California"); they understand that the universe will not implode without their constant attention. They still generally rebuff the American culture of multitasking (another word, by the way, that doesn't exist in the French lexicon). They don't dine with Bluetooths strapped on their ears. They aren't quick to hand out business cards unless they're really doing business. They know about essential things. That's why we love them. That's why everything seems sexier in France. "They invented sex during the day, lingerie, and the tongue," Bill Maher once said of the French. "Can't we admit we could learn *something* from them?"

French women know that like joie de vivre, *art de vivre* is not necessarily about attaining a state of sustained and sublime inner contentment; it's about the act of enjoying essential pleasures outside oneself—even despite oneself. Life is filled with innumerable imperfections after all, and *art de vivre* is not a cure for them. On the contrary, *art de vivre* is what makes life worth living with all of its pernicious complexities.

"Every French man and every French woman takes time to live, and has an extraordinarily clear and sound sense of what constitutes *Real Living*," Edith Wharton once wrote. Those are Wharton's italics, by the way, and they suggest a desire to distinguish Real Living—something authentic and intensely lived—from the surface production value of "entertaining" or the joyless perfections of, say, a Martha Stewart. Not to pick on poor Martha; that said, if Stewart is often construed as a model of *art de vivre* in America, she can hardly be called a paragon of bon vivantism, nor does she seem particularly inclined to embrace the virtues of letting your hair down. Let us not confuse *Good Housekeeping* icons with the virtues of savoir faire (know-how) and those of *savoir vivre* (social graces), both of which have little to do with the savory imperatives of *art de vivre* or Real Living.

Real Living is about the seductive attributes of simplicity, but, Reader, beware: when we confuse the culture of Real Living with the culture of, say, *Real Simple*—with its subtle endorsement of doing everything a bit more efficiently and better organized (and always in attractive matching airtight containers)—we're in trouble not only because efficiency and organization can quickly become one of those deadly virtues when we take them too seriously but also because Real Simple can get Real Complicated when Real Life gets in the way. It can also get Real Unsexy.

"Liberalism kills the libido" French writer Elisabeth Weissman once told me over the phone. We were talking about *art de vivre* and it was impossible to sweep this little detail under the rug. *Libéralisme* is a soft word in French for capitalism and the consumer culture that has created our particular American treadmill, and according to Weissman it's impossible to remove capitalism from our comparative love/sex equation. On the American side we're tenaciously work- and money-driven, incessantly on the move for the Next Big Thing. We fret over the unforeseen future and try not to fall through the cracks as the gap between the haves and have-nots grows even further apart. In short, we are brilliant at making a living but not quite sure how to have a life, because, never mind our faith, we all practice the Religion of Work.

Now French women *do* have their treadmill, and you'll often hear them complain about the nefarious effects of *métro-boulot-dodo* (commute-work-sleep) and other seriously unhappy conditions of living in a global economy. That said, by American standards they still live in a wildly sexy and extravagant culture. Imagine it: that thirty-five-hour workweek. Up to six weeks of paid vacation per year, plus numerous saint's days that miraculously fall on a Friday or a Monday. Subsidized child care and free preschools. National health care that frees the mind from the tyranny of medical bills and, more important, a culture that exalts Epicureanism, intellectualism, and bon vivantism.

Even more alluring benefits specifically designed to nurture their well-being await French women. For example, after giving birth, all French women enjoy free electro-Kegel rejuvenation sessions in order to "reeducate" and maintain the integrity of their vaginal floors. I didn't even know I had a vaginal floor until I gave birth in Paris. Who wouldn't feel a tad sexier with all this in place? In short, the French may flirt with atheism and existentialism but they still worship the Gods of Pleasure.

With these life-affirming social benefits in place, French couples live with less financial fear and stress than their

American counterparts—and what drives a stake through the libido more efficiently than fear and stress? In fact, if anything stresses French women these days, it's the looming threat to the sanctity of those social benefits, which sends thousands of them protesting in the streets with the same passion that sent them storming across Paris for Marie Antoinette's head. How lovely to live in a land where instead of paying lip service to family values, the government actually underwrites them (and women will put on their lipstick and get out to fight for them). I can't imagine anything that would set a similar scene in America short of a revolution—and, frankly, who's got the time for that?

I moved to Paris as a single woman, got married there, and had two kids. The French system and way of life became my point of reference. Of course, France is no cakewalk and life can become miserable in this old and sometimes crusty continental culture. But as journalist Judith Warner once pointed out, if things are better for women in France, it's because there exists "a profound and enduring social consensus that life should be made livable, based on who they are and not on an abstract moralistic notion of how they ought to be." The thought alone is so liberating, I'd like to burn my bra this very minute.

In France, the Gods of Pleasure enchant the French with enviable regularity, reminding them that All Work and No Play Makes Jacques a Dull Boy (and Gives Jeanette a Headache). In fact, when most Anglos are repenting for their holiday sins and excesses, the French, after weeks of serious holiday partying, do what appears to them as the most reasonable, logical thing to do: they keep partying.

January barely rolls out, for example, and the Gods get going with La Fête des Rois. This charming party tradition enjoyed by kids and grown-ups alike involves making a frangipane cake inside of which a small trinket called a *fève* is hidden. A *fève* is a bean that has been replaced these days by a tiny ceramic figurine of a king, and whoever finds this prize in their slice of cake gets to wear a gold paper crown and is king or queen for the day. The tradition of La Fête des Rois goes back to the Middle Ages and honors the day the three kings gave gifts to Jesus, but I believe the kings actually gave a gift to the French (the gift that keeps on giving): they gave them one more excuse to eat cake and drink champagne.

Now, French women might not get fat but American women end up looking like Eddie Murphy in *Norbit* if they're not careful. I spent my first holiday season in France in fear of this reality. I consumed spectacular amounts of sugar, butter, meat, and alcohol in the Loire Valley, as well as beasts that were feathered, cloven, or pecking at bits of frozen corn in the backyard the morning before they ended up as dinner. Breton bread puddings, blood sausages, and tripe found their way to my plate—on the same day. On one occasion I actually ate an entire sombrero-sized desert brioche ring studded with hot pink pralines. Guilt and gluttony were my holiday handmaidens.

- - - - - - - - -

Anticipating my whorish seasonal French bingeing all the way back in October, I'd taken out a lovely Clairefontaine writing pad and a cigar-sized cartridge pen filled with purple ink and written with great ceremony: NEW YEAR'S RESOLUTIONS. #1. DIET. (Nine other resolutions followed, since of course we must always have at least ten resolutions, don't ask me why.) Thus, as my French food fest began, there loomed like a dark halo around each meal the conviction that I'd spend half of the next year atoning. I'd eat nothing but yogurt and raw cucumbers and would do jumping jacks along the Seine with ten-pound weights in each hand.

I'd barely finished nursing my holiday hangover, however, when Chantal, a wiry and vivacious bookshop owner, invited me to her book-cluttered salon. "We are going to celebrate La Fête des Rois," she said.

"La fête des quoi?" I asked.

Frankly, I would have eaten a partridge in a pear tree at that moment to avoid eating more cake. But to say to Chantal and the group already gathered around her table (several spunky kids in gold paper crowns and their parents with champagne flutes in hand), *Sorry, folks, I've got a New Year's Resolution to respect here* would have made me a target of ridicule and contempt—and who needs that from the French?

Refusing to revel is a cultural misdemeanor in France. It singles you out as slightly Spartan. It is antipleasure. Moreover, the very term *New Year's Resolutions* sounds Conceptually Incorrect in France. There is no French idiom for it, in any case. The French will make a *voeu*, a wish, and that wish might include some sort of salubrious activity like getting in better shape. But a wish is a mutable thing that can be blown by the wind. A wish is like a cloud that might drift your way but that can't be forced to do so. It is languorous and fanciful and who knows where it will end up? A resolution, on the other hand, is a firm, concise obligation. It's a contract between You and Your Conscious that is deep-fried in moral values. A resolution has edges and they'll menace you forever if you don't pay attention to them. A resolution, in short, can become one of those deadly virtues if it conspires too radically against the Gods of Pleasure.

"This whole idea of New Year's Resolutions is very American," my friend Sandrine explains. "In general, in the French culture we are not taught to focus obsessively on long-term goals, to project ourselves into the future the way Americans do. That is also why we 'achieve less' "—here Sandrine made air quotes—"and why we have milder notions about ambition. In fact, ambition used to be frowned upon as something that can be hurtful, something that might hurt oneself or others, something that might compromise your quality of life. There is something supremely egocentric for the French tied in with ambition."

Ambition—another virtue that becomes a vice when taken too seriously. Time is not money for the French. It's an ephemeral currency and should be spent doing the things that make life worth living. Remember, the French woman might have acute sense of the brevity of time and the immediacy of pleasure; that said, she also has a strong predilection to enjoy not only the finer things in life but the things that make life fine. As Véronique Vienne put it, "Let's not confuse 'living well' with 'getting ahead.' " No, let's not. And while we're at it, let's not confuse the Good Life with having lots of stuff.

If the "good life" in France isn't associated with having lots of stuff, it's partly because money occupies a different place in the French frontal lobe. Which leads us to another cultural gap the size of Zurich. Suffice it to say, that if we Anglos are often hypocritical about sex, the French are often hypocritical about money. Where sex is morally dirty to many Anglos, money is morally dirty to many French people. Thus, a sex scandal will quickly be forgiven by the French but a financial one can taint a career and bury it forever. Despite its reputation for luxury, France remains a frugal country (a new world of revolving personal credit that's recently been introduced to the French could do more to undermine their *art de vivre* than all the French McDonald's combined, but I digress). Money is not inherently sexy to them. It is not a tool of seduction. The more you flaunt it, the less appealing you are. The glitz-and-glam aesthetic of the nouveau riche and the überrich is generally a turnoff. This partly explains why French women aren't quick to query a first date with the bullish: *So what do you do for a living?* This implies that what you do (i.e., what you make) is more important than who you are. In fact, in a poll of what French women look for in a mate, financial security was ranked as their lowest priority. How refreshing.

Less refreshing is the extent to which the Pursuit of Happiness in America is bound up in the size of one's wad, and how it leads to endless pileups in the fast lane. Is it any surprise, then, that the average American life sometimes seems like a great enterprise that needs constant negotiation, with couples often resembling business partners in a for-profit enterprise and trophy kids replacing trophy wives on the domestic mantelpiece? The have-it-all, do-it-all pressures of daily life, the lack of social benefits and all that fifty-fifty double-entry love accounting seem perfectly calibrated to knock the wind out of any good relationship. No wonder the sexless marriage has become such a big celebrity for Anglos. The Do-It-All modern woman, so everyone says, is doing everything but "It."

Regrettably, I, too, was swept up in the grind when I returned to the States. Managing daily life felt like setting Noah's ark off to sea on a daily basis, buoyed along by a slew of invisible perils and questions: When had parenting become a verb? Why was micromanaging life a new crusade? How did it come to pass that everything seemed like a job? I fondly recalled a time in Paris when having a life trumped making a living; when, despite heavy workloads, my husband and I still found the time to take what he called "siestas *crapuleuses*," or licentious naps. I do not believe further translation is necessary. In America, with its particular pressures and preoccupations, those little naps quickly became history. The Gods of Pleasure had gone on strike.

Now French women not only know how to entertain the Gods of Pleasure; many of them know how to make room for them despite the gorgeous chaos of children and the imperatives of making a living. Meet Geneviève. Geneviève is one of those women who popped her babies out like watermelon seeds and moved on to motherhood with the same ease, and she knows a bit about *art de vivre*. A case in point: After I gave birth in Paris, I baby-proofed our home with rubber edge liners, covers on electrical sockets, latches on windows, locks on drawers, and toilet seat guards. The parts of our living room that weren't bound and shackled were filled with happy, fluorescent kiddie toys. Geneviève took one look at our place and said, "Your apartment looks like a psych ward."

Geneviève's house was different: The kids had rules and boundaries. There was a place for their life and a place for mommy and daddy's life. The living room was a collective space, but it was a *grown-up* space, and the children learned to respect it as such. (How handy later in life!) The kids were in bed absolutely no later than 8:30 so that Mommy and Daddy could be together, because private time for Mommy and Daddy was very important. And Geneviève didn't pretend that Mommy and Daddy were going to bed to knit stockings and read the *Reader's Digest*. As she recalls, "One night when I was putting her to bed, my daughter asked, 'Are you and Daddy going to go in your room and kiss?' And I replied, 'Of course. Mommies and daddies kiss at night because they love each other. Now, nighty-night.' "

Her honesty threw me for a loop. "You mean, you just told her?"

"Why not? What is wrong with that? And do you not care to have any private life at all?"

I was reminded once again of Voltaire's suggestion that we must cultivate our own gardens. I was also reminded of the terribly unfeminist French expression, *Treat your husband like a lover and your wife like a mistress*. Certainly, a few well-placed boundaries are a great start. So is a living room that doesn't look like a psych ward.

Kids are not King in France (though you know something strange is going on when the French start naming their kids "Kevin" and "Cindy"). Where childhood trumps adulthood in the States, the opposite is largely true in France. The social consensus here is that children should be primed to live in the grown-up world, rather than have grown-ups prime themselves to adapt a wee bit too vigorously to the child's world. Here it's the young who take on a certain precocious worldliness. Most of them don't grow up with exclamations of *Great job!* buoying them along every milestone. To French women this is an annoying form of hyperbole; they're far less focused on *Just do it! You're the best!* and more inclined to shrug things off with a fatalistic and sometimes infuriating *It is not possible*. Even the French way of suggesting that something is really good is to say that it's *pas mal*—not bad.

Not the most ebullient and encouraging form of child-rearing, perhaps (the debate on that subject is a thorny thicket, indeed), but if French children grow up seeming almost adult in their sophistication it's partly because independence is bestowed upon them at an early age, and in ways that appear almost frightful to Anglos. But it's precisely this independence—or the ability of French women to let go and not fretfully micromanage and overprotect their children—that helps keep the blood pulsing through all that *art de vivre*.

French women, for example, frequently let their little ones go off at a young age to camps and to *sorties* at their grandparents' home. There is no guilt in this. (Guilt: the American woman's evil stepmother.) There is no Florida-style retirement equivalent in France, either, and French grandparents are often called upon to babysit for what would be considered lavish periods of time by American standards. This reinforces a certain old-fashioned family cohesion in France that contrasts starkly with family life in America, where we can all smirk in recognition at a recent *New Yorker* cartoon that featured an elderly couple in their car with a bumper sticker that reads: *Ask me about my estranged grandchildren*. And it also helps Mommy and Daddy have a life.

A case in point: Many years ago in Paris when I refused to let my son go to England on a three-day field trip with his bilingual preschool class, the nursery school director looked at me warily. "Madame," she said, "holding on to your child is not good for cultivating an independent spirit. You must let go and let your children venture into the world." Then she smiled (a bit smugly, I might add) and said, "We only have this problem with Anglo-Saxon mothers." And off went the children: The French kids left in rambunctious groups to travel across the English Channel, while the American kids returned home with their moms. The French mothers then enjoyed three lovely days alone with their hubbies in Paris to revel as they saw fit until little Jean or Claudette returned happy and healthy with tales from the English countryside. Meanwhile, the American moms lugged their gear and sand toys to a rainy park where they sat on the wet asphalt and, leery of the security hazards around them (swings with broken belts, precarious jungle gyms with no rubber mats), cheered everyone on with *Good job!* then went home, exhausted, and fell asleep with the kids.

SEX IS WHAT BROUGHT French women their kids in the first place; presumably it's what they're supposed to keep having in the second place. That said, you won't see many French women running off to workshops with "sex-enhancement specialists" or pole dancers, for while French women may find it odd when Americans speak of their children in ways that suggest an erotic transfer from husband to child, they find it equally bizarre when the other extreme is championed. French women generally aren't obsessed with their spouses any more than they're obsessed with their children. Here again we're back to living in that *juste milieu* where one extreme is not swapped for the other. French women live in the middle ground, not in the extremes. The tendency to compartmentalize, sensationalize, or otherwise lavish great heaps of concentrated emotional energy in husband or child is considered suspect. French women love their children madly like everyone else, of course, but children generally don't polarize them into either self-sacrificing übermothers or self-congratulatory Hot Mamas. In either extreme, the French woman smells a whiff of the female ghetto.

Children must be in the mix of life, imperatively. So, too, must men. When Edith Wharton writes that Real Living *à la française* is about "fundamental things," she describes these fundamental things as revolving "above all in close and constant and interesting and important relations between men and women." Close. Constant. Interesting. Important.

French women know that for true *art de vivre* to flourish, men must be *in* the picture, not out of it; the sacrilege of too much "homosociality" must be avoided. Women must arrange their chairs in boy-girl-boy-girl configurations and commingle with men, not necessarily as sexual partners, but as intellectual and social cohorts; as coconspirators in the game of life and not as cogs in the wheel of a domestic enterprise, or as annoying mammals who need to be trained to perform the tasks that we women so anxiously submit ourselves to.

Though we may not care to acknowledge this dark secret, we all know that nothing kills desire more swiftly than the wars fought on home turf as we micromanage our lives. And it's often on the home front, where sex lives and dies, that the problems begin; it's here, where we try to be all things to all people and shine the surfaces soiled by the messy paw prints of life, that another one of those saintly virtues becomes a vice: the notion that Cleanliness is Godliness.

Now this old dictum is often attributed to Saint Thomas Aquinas who, living roughly 800 years ago, did not enjoy the modern miracles of sanitation technology that we do. Though Saint Thomas was referring to moral purity when he spoke of cleanliness, I can't help but imagine how far a little hand sanitizer and room freshener would have gone back in the grubby thirteenth century. Be that as it may, for the purposes of this chapter, let us consider "cleanliness" in its broadest context. Let us consider it emblematic of all that modern housewifery that has such an evangelical vise grip on American women—all the cleaning, controlling, organizing, monitoring, planning, and micromanaging of life—or of everything that knocks the life out of *art de vivre*. In fact, let us suggest that such obsessive housewifery is likely to turn us into that cranky American woman on her godforsaken deserted island in the joke that debuted our chapter.

Who can deny the connection between appearance anxiety in all its expressions (what our homes look like, our kids, our husbands, ourselves) and the extent which we might feel (or not) like free agents of passion? Simone de Beauvoir had some interesting commentary to make on this point in *The Second Sex:* "Few tasks are more like the torture of Sisyphus than housework, with its endless repetition. . . . The battle against dust and dirt is never won. Washing, ironing, sweeping, ferreting out rolls of lint from under wardrobes—all this halting of decay is also the denial of life."

The denial of life. That's how much Simone de Beauvoir cared about the domestic drudgeries of housework.

On that note, I've rarely met a French woman who apologized for the state of her home—few French women who excuse the clutter in a living room, or a rumpled unmade bed, or the roused and aroused chaos of domestic life. Many French women are obsessed with aesthetics, but if they're wary of the aesthetics of housecleaning (or of the perfect couple or the perfect family), they seem equally wary of perfect order. I'm reminded of Penelope Green who, in writing about the anti-clutter movement, came right out with it: "It's a movement that confirms what you know deep down all along: really neat people are not avatars of the good life; they are humorless and inflexible prigs, and have way too much time on their hands."

Nothing against "really neat people" of course. What's compelling here is the notion that when a woman puts too much energy into the frenetic machinations of having a showroom life, she is, on some level, denying herself both the good life and an authentic life. As de Beauvoir suggests, "In a woman's war against dust, stains, mud, and dirt, she is fighting sin, wrestling with Satan," but life will rush on without her, and "the years no longer rise up toward heaven—they lie spread out ahead, gray and identical."

Ergo: women cannot be existentially or emotionally free if they must run in tight, frantic, and ultimately disappointing circles in their homes. They cannot be sexually free, either, it stands to reason. De Beauvoir, France's ultimate Dutiful Daughter, harvested her own brilliance and lived an authentic life by shaking off the duties that her social standing required of her, and to say that she had an enduring influence on French women is an understatement. We can attribute the defiant spirit of French women at least partly to the influence of de Beauvoir, who suggested that they do the one thing that most American women are taught *not* to do. For while we might deeply admire French women, they have something more delightfully incendiary to offer us than the cultural cream puffs thrown our way about how they look, cook, and don't get fat. What French women have to offer us when it comes to *art de vivre* is not how they elegantly negotiate the codes of the bourgeoisie but rather how they break those codes.

"We have broken the codes of the bourgeoisie," writer Michèle Fitoussi told me in speaking of what characterizes

- - - - - - - - -

French women. I've heard the same thing said by presidential candidate Ségolène Royal and by my sister-in-law, who lives in a small town in the middle of the French heartland. I'm sure if bourgeois bad girl Françoise Sagan were still around, she'd say the same thing, too. With its tentacles all wrapped up in de Beauvoir's defiance of social conventions, this assertion has been silently internalized in countless subtle ways in France, and it's at the root of what goes into genuine *art de vivre*.

Saying that you've broken the codes of the bourgeoisie is another way of saying that you don't care about doing things the "right way"; it's French-speak for suggesting that you don't believe in the virtues of the "perfect couple" or the perfect house, that you choose the sometimes messy attributes of letting go over the "denial of life" that de Beauvoir evoked. It's a way of suggesting that the world can stop, that you don't have to strategize or supersize your life, that you don't have to make the bed every day and you *can* press that Snooze button. In short, it's a way of Not Giving a Damn in the grandest sense of the term—a way of paying homage to the brevity of time and the immediacy of pleasure, come what may.

That is essentially the moral of a "life lesson" written by Erma Bombeck, a humorist whose work was as American as apple pie. Remarkably, Bombeck's essay "If I Had My Life to Live Over" keeps making regular appearances on the e-mail circuit, despite her heyday having passed decades ago, presumably because people still urgently need or want to hear its message.

Regrettably for Bombeck, her ode to living came at the end of her life, when the brevity of time had caught up with her, it was Bombeck's way of saying that if she'd had her life to live over she, too, would have broken the codes of the bourgeoisie.

Seven

BODY

On growing up laissez-faire about the body and the real reason (many—but not all) French women don't get fat

It's true that the French have a certain obsession with sex, but it's a particularly adult obsession. France is the thriftiest of all nations; to a French man, sex provides the most economical way to have fun.

—ANITA LOOS

In America sex is an obsession. In the rest of the world it's a fact.

—MARLENE DIETRICH

S everal years ago, a famous billboard campaign for a travel
company was launched in France. High above the streets
a young woman in a bikini stood proudly on a beach with her
hands on her hips. The caption read: NEXT WEEK, I'LL TAKE OFF MY
TOP. Motorists and pedestrians took note, and the following
week there she was—topless. (Her breasts, by the way, were
très French, which is to say that they were pert enough to fit
into the rim of a champagne glass.) Now that the company
had made good on its promise, the French would have gone
about their business inured to the topless titillation tower-
ing above them, but now the caption read: NEXT WEEK I'LL TAKE
OFF MY BOTTOMS. Now there *is* a limit to French nonchalance,
and this caused a great flurry of press—just as the marketers
had hoped. There was much pontification about advertising.
A few feminist groups sent out flares. But eventually things
settled into a state of bemused expectation.

The following week, the promise was delivered with a
denouement—only now our poster girl had turned around.

Instead of seeing full frontal nudity, we got her firm, free-wheeling derriere. Rabelaisian to the core, the French—men and women alike—essentially took it in good humor.

"I'm amused, not offended," a French girlfriend remarked in a statement that pretty much sums up another huge cultural gap between France and the United States. One need only evoke Janet Jackson's Super Bowl "wardrobe malfunction" to drive that point home. The fleeting sight of Jackson's bejeweled booby took on national security risk proportions, and in her armadillo-meets-Darth-Vader outfit (now *that* was true cause for alarm), Jackson unhinged an entire nation.

Now we can spill much ink on the *why* of it all—as in why in the world do we still live with the wiggy perversions and curious contradictions of puritanism—but let's stick with that billboard babe. Here we have the ultimate va-va-voom stereotype of the French woman, one that burst into the world most nakedly with Brigitte Bardot in Roger Vadim's *And God Created Woman*. Needless to say, most French women don't look like Bardot in her prime, and they're not likely to strip down and flash their French flesh lackadaisically to an entire nation. Still, the enduring cliché simply won't go away. I'm reminded of a recent *New Yorker* cartoon: an American man, woman, and boy look up at a painting of a naked woman in a museum. Mother: *She's not naked, Jake—she's French.*

As I drove through Paris and saw that billboard all over the city, it struck me (and here's another one of those elegant French paradoxes for you) that in her total nakedness that *femme* high above the streets was neither hard-core nor overtly sexual. She simply looked *"bien dans sa peau"*—or at ease in her own skin, a state of grace that is universally admired about French women. When you're *"bien dans ta peau,"* you're not only at ease with your body; you're at ease with your inner cargo. You're comfortable, in other words, with your Self.

But as is the case with many things French, there's a pernicious little subtext here. For this spiritual sister of Bardot was a reminder that looking and feeling good in one's skin is as much a civic duty in France as flirtation; she was also a visual prompt for French women, a reminder of that to which they should all aspire. And here we come to our paradox about French women. For while they are indeed less likely than us to conform to a single standard of beauty—while they embody the attributes of being *jolie laide* and assert a certain delectable personal iconoclasm—there *is* one standard that French women respect with an almost ecclesiastical rigor; there is one rule that they will almost all unanimously and silently obey, and it's a driving force behind all that sexy, French svelteness.

For what's the *real* reason French women don't get fat? Yes, we know they eat sanely, with great pleasure, and in moderation. But, ladies, let's cut to the chase: French women don't get fat because it is undeniably, unequivocally not okay to be fat in France. This social consensus, which is inextricably woven up in their perceptions of womanhood and sexiness, is so deeply ingrained in and stridently endorsed by French women that they will not mince words when they see any sign of creeping corpulence. All trademark discretion is set aside and instead of "You look fine" (or worse, "You look *great!*") when in fact you've gained fifteen pounds and look like a zeppelin, the French woman will go right for the jugular. "*Ma chérie*, how many kilos did you put on over the winter?" she'll ask. Or "*Attention!* That extra croissant will make you fat." That chorus might include your sister, your parents, your best friend, and possibly the manager of your apartment building. Even Mireille Guiliano of *French Women Don't Get Fat* fame brought that point home in the beginning of her book: When she returned to France after gaining heaps in America, her father took one look at her and said, "You look like a sack of potatoes." Welcome home.

If this ruthless but realistic honesty doesn't keep you fretting over body fat, a veritable onslaught of advertising will. Take a look at any French women's magazine, preferably just after winter when postholiday, foie gras–induced poundage must be shed in anticipation of summer nakedness, and you'll find a profusion of advertisements for products that combat cellulite (national enemy number one) and sagging body parts of all size and shapes. There are potions, pills, creams, gels, scrubs, serums, oils, kits, mitts, and electrical gadgets; there is drainage, lymphage, firmage, saggage, electrowattage, hypnosis, and other things that sound medically unsound. Larger-than-life, perfectly trim yet opulent *fesses* (that's French for ass) greet you at every pharmacy and, yes, on every billboard.

If you still don't get the point and you're feeling lonely and fat and want company, you will have a hard time finding solace, because the French do not possess the same Anglo-Saxon love of groups and associations and the general need to belong. You won't find, for example, magazines devoted to obscure groups (a magazine, say, for single, gay, Buddhist, vegetarian, over-forty, West Coast skydivers, no matter how charming or numerous they might be). Nor will you find a plus-size industry that will cater to what the French might perceive as Your Royal Bigness. If you're over a size 42 (a size 14 in the UK)—you might have to go to a specialized shop where, like the child in days of yore who bore the humiliation of buying freakishly large orthopedic shoes, you must submit yourself to a shopping experience that will haunt you for years to come.

If French women don't get fat—if, in fact, they look an awful lot like our naked siren on her billboard high above French streets—it's largely because fat is demonized in France, for better and for worse. That said, as fast food creeps into France and eating habits change, French women *are* starting to tip the scales. One quick trip outside Paris makes that quite clear. But until size 12 becomes the national norm or France becomes fat-friendly (two highly unlikely scenarios), French women will remain seriously svelte, and God help those who, contrary to popular opinion, *do* get fat.

- - - - - - - - -

Living in mortal fear of getting fat is anxiety we can all relate to, but the upside to this social pressure for French women (if we can call it an "upside") is that they will stoically battle the urge for short-term gratifications with the promise of those long-term pleasures and the undeniable sexiness that comes from feeling and looking good in one's skin. "I ate enough for four people," my friend Francine invariably shrieks after a big meal, before telling us how she will eat like a bird the following week to "deflate." And so she does, with a vengeance. "I do not want to become a French fatty!" she proclaims. Francine, bless her very small bones, is a particularly garrulous French woman who will readily express what most French women will generally keep to themselves, for fear of appearing what they indeed are, which is deeply alarmed by the prospect of getting fat.

"I think we're all the same," Francine once said. "It's just that French women are better at refusing to eat that little extra cookie. American women find a way to justify it." Or as Mireille Guiliano puts it: "The mind is the French woman's ultimate firewall against getting fat." In other words, the real secret is not what French women eat but how they get their wills of steel, that mental willpower, that sangfroid, the ability to reject the emotional comforts of food, and Just Say *Non!* to a chocolate éclair.

Or we can look at it this way: it's their ability to Just Say *Oui* to all those culinary pleasures—the frangipane cakes in Janu-

ary, the tarts and cassoulets and meringues and fresh bread—
and then carry out their private campaigns of strict culinary
abstinence afterward with such valiant determination.
"When you add an indulgence," Guiliano forewarns, "make
a corresponding reduction to compensate. Add another half
hour of walking. Skip the cocktail. Pass the bread basket." In
other words, atone. Or, at the very least, moderate yourself.
Thus Francine will push aside the nuts and assorted savory
goodies in a salad and let them pile up in a dejected mouth-
watering mound on her plate without so much as picking at
one lonely olive. Personally, I don't know what's more painful: watching such fabulous food go to waste or trying not to
spear one of those alluring olives off Francine's plate when
she's not looking.

It certainly helps that French culture is not a snack culture. When the evils of snacking are wired into your brain—
when snacking seems as nasty to a French girl as porn might
seem to an American girl—you grow up not grazing. The
kitchen might be a holy shrine in France but the French won't
genuflect in front of the refrigerator on a regular basis. Until
recently, you couldn't even find snack food near cash regis-
ters in retail environments in France. In fact, the first time
I saw a Parisian shamelessly snacking on chips in the metro,
I—me, a self-confessed American snack queen (I am eating a multigrain sesame garlic cracker as I write this)—was
shocked.

- - - - - - - - - -

Americans live in a feel-good culture that's rooted in the pleasures of short-term gratifications and creature comforts. American has also become a fat-friendly nation despite the obsession with weight loss, partly because there's plus-size cash to be made in the plus-size industry, and partly because we genuinely want everyone to feel good. Thus, there is a new entertainment culture devoted to the carnally endowed, with catwalks and TV shows that exalt "phat girlz" and "big babes" (right next to weight-loss reality shows like *The Biggest Loser*). But while there might be something empowering about voluminous vixens who unapologetically claim their bodies, the cruel reality is that there is no place for them in the French woman's world. If we look at the world through a French woman's eyes—a French woman, I might add, who does not come from a "feel good" culture and who wouldn't have a clue what you're talking about if you tried to explain the concept—being fat is a grave social misdemeanor. As my friend Marie put it, "You cannot feel good in your skin when you have too much of it. It is as simple as that. That's why French women are always amazed to see really heavy American women wearing shorts and not caring what people think. This is an aesthetic problem for us. Maybe we French are too narcissistic. I don't know. But even though you can admire an American women who can feel 'good in her skin' when she is fat, everyone knows that she would feel much better and a lot sexier in her skin if she weren't. In France, everyone will let her know that one way or the other."

IF OUR EYES ARE windows to our souls, our breasts must be gateways to our anxieties about womanhood. And American girls enter these gateways at an early age, often when they're introduced, with great ceremony, to their first training bra. Now, I don't know about you, but I have never considered the term "training bra" very, well, uplifting. The very word "training" implies that our breasts—like, say, the cheetah in a zoo—must be trained to live and be happy within the confines of a tight space, and that without that tight space things might get a little . . . wild. It implies that there is a right way for a breast to look and that, without being strapped into the appropriate cup size (which, by default, will train our breasts to grow into that right shape), our breasts will forever look wrong. This, of course, is not to deny the undeniable exhilaration that can also accompany the purchase of one's first training bra. I recall the flush of grown-up sexiness that came with mine—and the silent conviction that the purpose of the bra was not so much to wear it but to inspire someone to take it off.

Be that as it may, the "training bra" belies the very utilitarian attitude we Anglos have about our bodies. In contrast, of course, to the French. For starters, if you ask for a training bra in France, you will get a quizzical expression and then you will perhaps be shown a sports bra, but no one will

----

understand what you're referring to because the training bra—the thing, the concept—does not exist in France. The idea, if you try to explain it, sounds preposterous to them. At the first flush of bosomy expansion, a young French girl will go to a department store or to one of those intimate local lingerie boutiques you see all over France where the saleswoman knows more about the secrets of lingerie than any other human on earth. There might be a few men there as well, shopping with their women and inspecting merchandise with similar scrutiny. (What a revelation: French men, many of them as macho as they come, know about lingerie the way they know about cooking a *gigot d'agneau*.) This young girl will end up with a little satin pink polka-dot bra or a cat-print Princesse Tam-Tam bra, and it will have nothing to do with training anything whatsoever other than an eye for aesthetic flair.

If a marriage of pleasure and aesthetics informs the French relationship to the body more than one of utility and comfort, it could very well be woven up in the fibers of a girl's first bra. French women do indeed invest huge chunks of personal income in lingerie, and wherever you go in whatever French city, you're likely to be greeted by a perfectly shaped orb, compliments of La Perla, Aubade, or Chantelle. Even the tiniest little Monoprix grocery store in the most obscure town will have lots of lacy, racy lingerie to choose from. The modest Monoprix in our neighborhood in Paris, for example, is filled with aisles of lingerie that are prominently displayed in the *front* of the store. Groceries—food, diapers, water, the stuff you might need for actual sustenance—are located in the very back of the store, as if they were an afterthought.

Now, true confessions: my cup runneth over at an early age. I developed a pair of those big American breasts that were lampooned by those "two wild and crazy guys" in the *Saturday Night Live* skit back in what now seems like the Pleistocene era. Training bras were essentially useless. I actually needed (here's a great word for you) armature. I recall one particularly embarrassing fitting session with my mother when she discovered the ultimate support sports bra back in its heyday. This bra had more armor than a jeep. It had steel underwire and huge padded straps and reinforced cups. It looked like it could withstand severe windstorms and an occasional meteor shower.

All this to say that utilitarian comfort would most definitely describe the nature of my relationship to my own body as a young girl, never mind my introduction to lingerie. I could relate to actress Gilda Radner, who once said, "I base most of my fashion taste on what doesn't itch." This did not, however, deter me from trying to find the perfect French bra when I first moved to Paris. I went to the Galeries Lafayette which, with its spectacular dome and gilded terraces, feels a little like walking into a giant jewelry box. Amid the splendor and the cacophony of this majestic department store I tried on bras in every brand, size, and fabric. I tried them on in silk, satin, cotton, and tulle. I tried them on with lace-scalloped edges, bows and polka dots, velvet trim and spandex. I pushed and prodded until I came to the sobering conclusion that nothing fit. Weary, I took my big American breasts to a local café and together we nursed a much-needed drink.

Beyond this rhapsody in 34C, there's something more basic to appreciate about the French, which is their ability to experience less guilt and moral hand-wringing about the body. They enjoy carnal virtues as an integral part of life, the same way they might enjoy a good meal (*"Il bouffe bien, il boit bien, il baise bien"*—he eats well, he drinks well, he fucks well— is a common French saying that pretty much sums up that idea). The sweaty palms of puritanism have not manhandled French culture; the weight of Protestant guilt doesn't bog the people down.

Nowhere does this reality more flagrantly defy our norms than when children come into the picture. A strange thing happened, for example, not long after we returned to the States one summer. I was speaking to a friend over dinner one night when my son looked up at me with a flustered expression. "Mom," he stammered. "You said a bad word." My younger daughter chimed in. "Yeah, Mom, you said a Really Super Totally Bad Word." I didn't know what they were talking about until my friend mentioned that I had said the "S word" in front of the kids. The word "sex."

The more I tried to reason with my kids about the "not bad" implications of the word, the more "bad" it seemed (and the more embarrassed my kids became). It got so off-putting that at one point when my son asked me the title of this book while I was writing it, I replied, "What French women know about love and . . . *stuff*." Not much time had gone by since we'd left France, but culturally we'd traversed light-years. How, I wondered, did a word with no great moral charge associated with it in France become "bad" to my children? What insidious cultural messages had been beamed into their little brains? I recall looking on in horror one day when they joined a group of American kids who were taunting two naked toddlers on a California beach. The toddlers' parents, it turns out, were clueless Swedes who couldn't fathom the depth of discomfort that the sight of a naked body (even if it belonged to a four-year-old) could inflict on American children. You'd be hard-pressed to see a similar situation play out in France.

All of which harks back to what Charlotte Rampling suggested: If French women seem more laissez-faire about the business of the body, it's in great measure because French culture has *made* them that way. In other words, they *grow up* that way. Literally.

It's no news that in France nakedness abounds. You can't walk through a park or past a civic monument in France without seeing a bronze breast or pair of buttocks. You can't walk through any museum without seeing the naked body represented in all its glory. People kiss on the streets and on park benches; fun fairs typically feature scenes of cartoonish bacchanalia painted across the tops of bumper cars, rides, and amusement arcades (buxom women bursting out of their corsets or doing the cancan in Day-Glo bordellos; cartoon men with their eyeballs popping out of their heads in carnal delight). It's often simultaneously smutty and funny, bawdy and burlesque, and parents don't rush their children away or avert any eyes.

My favorite affirmation, however, about the way French children grow up surrounded by the realities and fancies of the carnal world came when my son was barely a toddler. One day, his friend Natasha approached me in excitement. She had a new doll. It looked semireal and had a trademark name: Fanfan. Natasha was enamored with Fanfan not only because it was a popular doll for her age group but because it had a nifty little feature: it peed. With the fierce pride of someone who'd just discovered a new phylum of animal life, she lifted up its tiny faux diapers to show me. "Look!" she declared. And, indeed, little Fanfan tinkled away. But what surprised me were not the little drops of water, or faux "pee-pee"; it was the doll's gender. Fanfan, it turns out, was a boy doll, and he had a tiny anatomically correct plastic penis to prove it.

I must have gasped, or maybe I blurted out in French, "Well, will you *look* at that . . ." because Natasha looked at me with a worried expression, then back at Fanfan and asked, "What's wrong?" Where do I begin? I felt like asking. At the time, the Fanfan doll was distributed by the French doll company Corolle, owned by Mattel, but you won't find this one anatomically correct feature on any Fanfan doll in your local toy store because, as the director of North American operations for Corolle put it: "The mass market is reticent to sell sexed dolls. . . . The United States is still a puritanical society. Sex is something that Americans don't want out in the open."

Here's a statement so dripping with paradox and irony, we won't even go near it, other than to suggest the obvious: what's considered "sexed" to Americans is considered simply part of life to the French. Thus, many of the educational toys and books that introduce the French child to the body go through a wash-and-spin cycle before they reach American shores—*if* they ever reach those shores, that is.

Take the elegant toddler Louvre museum book simply called *Breasts*, which features memorable mammaries by masters like Goya, Gauguin, and Botticelli and which begins with "When I grow up, I'm going to have breasts just like Mommy." Or two classic children's books published by Gallimard in their famous *Mes Premières Découvertes* (My First Discoveries) series called *Before Birth* and *Birth*, which use animals to explain the basics of reproduction. Here a vast cross section of the animal kingdom is depicted in small, graphically correct illustrations at (fore)play, mating, brooding, and being born. Both books were strewn on the floor of our apartment in Paris when an American friend picked them up and commented, "You'd never see books like this in the States." As it turns out, she was right. These books were launched at Frankfurt's book fair but, as one Gallimard editor said with a touch of tempered incredulity, "They were extremely well received by all publishers except the

- - - - - - - - -

Americans, who categorically refused them on the grounds that they were erotic."

A similar fate met another another Gallimard book called *The Body*. A bio-anatomy lesson for kids, the book features a boy, a girl, and a baby, with plastic overlays that illustrate everything from molecules to intestinal tracts. The French edition features nonsexual illustrations of two naked toddlers. In the American edition, the toddler has diapers on and the girl wears pants. In an ironic twist of global dimensions, this particular Gallimard book was distributed with no design modifications in roughly ten countries, including South Korea and Taiwan. This made America the only country in the world except for Islamic nations such as Iran (which banned circulation of the French 100-franc bill because it featured Delacroix's bare-breasted Liberty) to censor or modify material of this kind. With a certain strain in his voice, Arthur Hubschmid, the editorial director at French children's book publisher L'Ecole des Loisirs, summed up what seems to be a general consensus among Europeans: "Americans systematically censor anything that is vaguely scatological or sexual. [Anglo-Saxon] children's books live in a nursery ghetto where man is good and sex does not exist."

BACK IN 1957, French philosopher and semiotic adventurer Roland Barthes wrote: "The adult French man sees the child as another self. All the toys [in France] one commonly sees are essentially a microcosm of the adult world; they are all reduced copies of human objects. . . . The fact that French toys *literally* [Barthes' italics] prefigure the world of adult functions obviously cannot but prepare the child to accept them all, by constituting for him even before he can think about it, the alibi of Nature."

Barthes was onto something, wasn't he? Could it stand to reason that children who grow up with the realities of the body are primed to be less childlike and more matter-of-fact about sexuality as adults? Could it be that this offsets the extremes in America, where we swing on a vine between hard-core voyeurism and tee-hee giggliness about the body?

It only seems fitting to give Edith Wharton the last word at this point, not only because so many of her observations dust these pages but because the time in which she made those observations was so seminal. Wharton moved to Paris in the late nineteenth century and lived there until her death a few years before World War II. At no other time in history did so many Americans pour into France; at no other time did so many American *men*—many of them corn-fed boys who'd never been off the farm or out of their small towns—flood into the fields of France and into the arms of French women.

There was, admittedly, a lot of *voulez-vous coucher avec moi?* going on. War has a way of stripping human need to its most essential. And yet if French women introduced American men to carnal knowledge in ways they'd never experienced back home with Madge or Betty, it was in large measure because they, too, had their own emotional and existential hunger to feed. "It was a time when life and death were heightened," says Marie-Claude, a French senior citizen who lived through World War II as a young woman. "Our French men were away fighting, or dead, or in prison, or they came home dismembered. There was little food; there was no joy, only despair. For years, French women had been starved of love and sex, and so had American soldiers. These American GIs came to our devastated land with chocolates, cigarettes, nylons, chewing gum, canned food, lighters, and the most seductive thing of all: freedom. Is it any wonder that we French women opened our arms?"

The decades that followed World War II were a drinking binge of cultural change; that said, the French reputation for exalting the fleeting pleasures of passion has remained iconic over time. This undoubtedly accounts for the enormous enduring appeal of Robert Doisneau's postwar photograph "Le Baiser de l'Hôtel de Ville." Here we have the most famous French kiss on the planet: a Parisian couple lean into a swooning embrace that's become the ultimate postcard cliché of Frenchiness, but if I evoke it here, it's because it embodies the keen sense of the brevity of time and the immediacy of pleasure that we described earlier in these pages as a defining feature of the French woman's élan vital.

Both the urgency and the ordinariness of life glimmer

in Doisneau's photo. Our French couple is as insouciant of passersby as they are of them: a stern bespectacled man in a beret walks behind them, oblivious to their embrace; a woman in a trench coat stares off into the hazy distance, lost in thought. Others pass in the streets, smoke in bistros, amble past the city's Hôtel de Ville, which looks much the same way now as it did then, with the same brasseries, the same dull pigeon gray sky, the same noisy rumbling of the gears of life. Wars might come and go, people are born and die, but the French, Doisneau's photo seems to say, will always find time for love and sex.

Though Doisneau shot that image thirteen years after Wharton died, her insight into the transcendent gifts of the French still rings true. And so with the last word on what French women know about love, sex, and other matters of the heart and mind, we turn one last time to Wharton, who with trademark acuity wrote of the French: "From their freedom of view combined with their sensuous sensibility they have extracted the sensation they call *'le plaisir,'* which is something so much more definite and more evocative than what we mean when we speak of pleasure. *'Le plaisir'* stands for the frankly permitted, the freely taken, delight of the senses, the direct enjoyment of the fruit of the tree called golden. No suggestions of furtive vice degrade or coarsen it, because it has, like love, its open place in speech and practice. . . . [T]o the French it is part of the general fearless and joyful contact with life."

- - - - - - - - -

IS THAT A BAGUETTE IN
YOUR POCKET OR ARE YOU
JUST HAPPY TO SEE ME?

"It's a new French revolution!" Sonia Rykiel's daughter, Nathalie, announced about Rykiel Woman, France's first upscale sex-toy boutique. "It's a way to display eroticism and create desire." That said, after much fanfare there wasn't much desire in sight, and the boutique had a desultory feeling about it from the get-go, as if the *air du temps* had already lost its air. Despite their ooh-la-la reputation, French women simply weren't storming *la boutique* for the latest designer sex toy. *Qu'est-ce qui se passe?*

"The French find sex toys too mechanical," a spokesperson for Chambre 69 (France's first upscale sex Web site) told me. "There's this persistent idea that if you have to use a sex toy, you don't really know how to experience pleasure with another person or give it to another person. Maybe it's a question of pride, but French people are not able to get past the mechanical aspect of it all; they are slow to get beyond the fact that sex toys are purely utilitarian."

Slow indeed. According to a poll conducted by French *Elle* on the use of sex toys, "72 percent [of French women] don't see the utility of a little vibrating duck." As if to prove that point, the illustrious magazine of all things *femme* recently put four of its female editors to the test. The result?

Tester number one was reluctant to acknowledge the efficacy of her tiny vibrating Sonia Rykiel lipstick but eventually conceded "since it's much smaller than a fake penis, it's tempting to throw it in your purse and use it when you've got downtime, even if I'm astonished to be writing this very sentence."

Tester number two wrote of her experience with a remote-controlled minivibrator: "At first glance it looks like an egg, except that it's in mauve-colored plastic, like an Air Wick room freshener." Concerned that she might look "a bit moronic" using it, she remained unimpressed.

Not just unimpressed but unhinged by her Geisha Balls, our third tester wrote: "First, [they were] delivered without a user manual. . . . What to do with those two golf balls connected by a plastic umbilical cord?" After trying the product out ("visually it was a catastrophe; it looked like I'd grown a pair of gonads overnight"), fumbling with both orifices ("huh. . . ?") and getting annoyed by "these little balls inside the big balls that sound like maracas," our user gave up. "*Pfft*, it's too complicated."

Our fourth and final tester was given a dildo that "looks like a black rubber banana." Fretting about where to buy the batteries for the gizmo, she later broke out in a sweat at the prospect of actually finding her G-spot with a large faux fruit. "I am vaguely disturbed by the idea of ending up in an emergency Intensive Care unit." Panicked, she removed the batteries when her boyfriend arrived. Of her warm-blooded Homo sapiens partner, "Bothered by Banana" told her readers: "Between you and me, when it comes to sex toys there's nothing better."

About the Author

Debra Ollivier lived in France for ten years, during which time she married her French husband and had two children. She was a frequent contributor to Salon.com and *Le Monde*, and her work has apppeared in *The Guardian*, *Playboy*, *Les Inrockuptibles*, and *Harper's*. She is also the author of *Entre Nous: A Woman's Guide to Finding Her Inner French Girl*. Ollivier lives with her family in Los Angeles and Paris.